Approaching Pipe Rolls

This is the first study specifically concerned with thirteenth-century pipe rolls and shows how pipe rolls were compiled, what they contain, and how to read them.

These records of English government finance were produced annually. They list debts owed to the government, by the sheriffs of each county, by manors and boroughs, and by individuals for taxes, fines and judicial penalties. They also list the payments made, sometimes in cash to the treasury, sometimes for building works, fees for royal employees and relatives, the provision of castles, and much more. The rolls are an essential source for administrative history, and provide detailed information for family and local historians. All the rolls are now readily available, either in print or online, but they are at first sight difficult to understand.

This book shows how the rolls evolved in the course of the century and serves as a guide for beginners, armed with some basic Latin, who want to explore these records. As well as explaining the conventions of dates, numbers, abbreviations, monetary units and so on, it illustrates the material to be found in pipe rolls by a detailed examination of a single roll.

Richard Cassidy has a PhD degree in medieval history from King's College, London. He is the author of numerous articles on government finance and administration in England and Ireland in the thirteenth century. His edition of the 1259 pipe roll is to be published in 2024.

Approaching Medieval Sources

Approaching Pipe Rolls
The thirteenth century

Approaching Pipe Rolls
The Thirteenth Century

Richard Cassidy

LONDON AND NEW YORK

First published 2024
by Routledge
4 Park Square, Milton Park, Abingdon, Oxon OX14 4RN

and by Routledge
605 Third Avenue, New York, NY 10158

Routledge is an imprint of the Taylor & Francis Group, an informa business

© 2024 Richard Cassidy

The right of Richard Cassidy to be identified as author of this work has been asserted in accordance with sections 77 and 78 of the Copyright, Designs and Patents Act 1988.

All rights reserved. No part of this book may be reprinted or reproduced or utilised in any form or by any electronic, mechanical, or other means, now known or hereafter invented, including photocopying and recording, or in any information storage or retrieval system, without permission in writing from the publishers.

Trademark notice: Product or corporate names may be trademarks or registered trademarks, and are used only for identification and explanation without intent to infringe.

British Library Cataloguing-in-Publication Data
A catalogue record for this book is available from the British Library

ISBN: 978-1-032-31335-1 (hbk)
ISBN: 978-1-032-31336-8 (pbk)
ISBN: 978-1-003-30926-0 (ebk)

DOI: 10.4324/9781003309260

Typeset in Sabon
by Apex CoVantage, LLC

Contents

Introduction   1

1   Pipe rolls for beginners   3
What is a pipe roll? 3
How to begin 5
Language 6
Abbreviations 7
Headings 8
Numbers 8
Money 9
Dates 11

2   The rolls system and background   15
Historical background 15
The rolls system 16
Chancellor's rolls 17
Pipe rolls on parchment 18
Pipe rolls in print 19
Pipe rolls online 20
Dialogue of the Exchequer 21
Literature about pipe rolls 22

3   Pipe roll contents   29
Debts and payments 29
The sheriff's account 30
Farm, increment, and profit 31
Manors and boroughs 33
Amercements 34
Fines and offerings 35

Taxes 35
Introducing the foreign accounts 38
What's in the foreign accounts? 40
What's not in the pipe rolls 42

4   **An example: the 1259 pipe roll**   46

The example, and where to find it 46
A county account: Northamptonshire 47
Details of the county account 49
The roll and revenue 50
County farm and profit 52
Fines in 1259 53
Profits of justice 54
Pipe roll timetable 55
Pipe rolls and receipt rolls 57
Pipe roll and memoranda roll accounts 59
The pipe roll and current events 60
The pipe roll and local and family history 61

5   **Pipe rolls in the thirteenth century**   67

Too much information 67
Reducing new entries 68
Reducing old entries 70
Pipe rolls and other rolls 73

Appendix 1 Transcription examples   77
Oxfordshire account, 1237 pipe roll 78
Oxfordshire account, 1293 pipe roll 79
Appendix 2 Glossary   82
References   86
Index   93

Introduction

My own introduction to pipe rolls happened twenty years ago, when I was an MA student at King's College London. I had the good fortune to be taught by David Carpenter, who explained why pipe rolls were important, and how to make sense of the printed editions produced by the Pipe Roll Society. He later supervised my PhD thesis, an edition of the 1259 pipe roll. At that time, the only way to see an unpublished pipe roll was in person, at The National Archives in Kew. There I spent many days, struggling with cumbersome parchment rolls. I can still recall the sinking sense of despair I felt when first unrolling an actual pipe roll, and the dread that I would never be able to understand the handwriting, the abbreviations, and the accounting conventions. In writing this book, I have tried to remember that sensation, and not to take anything for granted, in order to help readers who are themselves encountering pipe rolls for the first time.

Since I first visited The National Archives, there has been a revolution in accessibility. Photographs of the unpublished pipe rolls, and many other records, are freely available to anyone with an internet connection, thanks to the Anglo-American Legal Tradition website. You no longer have to go to Kew to be faced with a vast and baffling mass of thirteenth-century Latin. You can be baffled in the comfort of your own home. But with a little perseverance, and some basic knowledge of Latin, you can unlock the contents of the pipe rolls. Few of the rolls from the years after 1226 have been published, and there is no doubt much still to be found within them. They offer insights into almost every aspect of English government finance and administration. They are also major sources for local and family history. The information they contain is just waiting to be explored. I hope that this book will help explorers find their way.

The book covers a lot of technical topics, with some specialized vocabulary. I have tried to explain terms as they are introduced, but there is also a glossary at the end, to provide occasional reminders. All the unpublished rolls mentioned are held by The National Archives (TNA), and they are referred to by their TNA catalogue numbers. References to unpublished pipe rolls and memoranda rolls include notes of the relevant image numbers on

DOI: 10.4324/9781003309260-1

2 *Introduction*

the Anglo-American Legal Tradition website, so that readers can see for themselves what I am talking about (and perhaps disagree).

I learned a lot about pipe rolls and other sources from informal reading groups with my fellow MA and PhD students at King's College London, and from seminars at the Institute of Historical Research. I could not have completed a thesis, let alone written a book about pipe rolls, without this network of helpful and learned medieval historians.

1 Pipe rolls for beginners

At its simplest, a pipe roll was a list of debts to the medieval English government, together with any payments towards these debts. This sounds straightforward, but reading and understanding pipe rolls can be a daunting prospect at first. There is no point in pretending otherwise: pipe rolls can seem quite forbidding, whether you meet them in person, in print, or online. But they are really not as bad as they look. They are for the most part formulaic and repetitive; this means that, once you have got used to the set terminology and scribal habits, they can be read quite easily. The language is generally simple, and there is a limited repertoire of conventional abbreviations. The difficult part is becoming accustomed to the basic elements which make up the rolls. From then on, much of the content of pipe rolls will fall into place as no more than a series of repetitions of familiar phrases. The printed transcripts at least take care of the abbreviations, but they still leave the reader with the problems of language and accounting conventions. This chapter deals with the process of reading an actual roll, or a photo of one, or a printed edition, and the conventions which are likely to baffle readers, until they have got used to the practices of the thirteenth-century Exchequer.

What is a pipe roll?

Each year, for some seven hundred years, a pipe roll was produced by the Exchequer, the department of the English government concerned with finance. The production of the rolls was linked to a process by which officials' accounts were subjected to an audit examination. These officials included the sheriffs who ran the administration of the counties and collected the debts due to the central government.

The pipe rolls listed sums owed and paid. The debts could be those owed by private individuals, for taxes, fines, or penalties imposed by the courts. Other debts were owed collectively, by cities, boroughs, or manors. The debts could also be sums due from officials working for the government, such as the sheriffs themselves, or the administrators of the royal forests; in the thirteenth century, administrators were generally held individually responsible for the revenues produced in their area of responsibility, and such debts were pursued from them and their heirs even after they left office or died.

When payments had been made against these debts, in part or full, these were recorded in the pipe roll. Some payments were simply paid into the Treasury, the department of the Exchequer which handled the cash which the government received, stored, and paid out. Other amounts were paid out locally by officials, as instructed by the central government, drawing on the revenues which they had collected. Unpaid debts were copied into the following year's pipe roll, so that they would not be forgotten, and could be repeated in successive pipe rolls for many years.

Each year's debts and payments were audited and recorded in large parchment rolls. These rolls were generally known in the thirteenth century as rolls of the year, *rotuli annales*, or as 'great rolls'; 'great' could refer both to their size and to their importance. Physically, they were certainly large and cumbersome. The rolls were made up of membranes of sheepskin parchment. Each membrane was ruled with about eighty horizontal lines, and two vertical lines near the left margin to accommodate the capital letter at the beginning of each entry. Two of these membranes were stitched head to tail, to make a rotulet – a section of a larger roll. Each rotulet in the earliest surviving roll, from 1130, was about 300 mm wide and up to 1200 mm long. By the mid-thirteenth century, the rotulets had grown and were up to 400 mm wide and 1500 mm long (the size of membranes tended to increase in the thirteenth century, perhaps because of the introduction of larger breeds of sheep). For the most part, entries were written in a single wide column, with a narrow left margin, and often written right up to the right edge of the membrane.

Each year, such rotulets were used to record outstanding debts, copied from the previous year, mostly listed by county. New debts were added at the end of each county's account. The payments for the year were checked and filled in as the audit process took place over several months. When the audit was complete, the rotulets for the year were all gathered together, and sewn together at the head, to make the full roll. When rolled up, a rotulet looked rather like a cylindrical tube, and was sometimes called a pipe. A complete roll looks still more like a section of pipe, particularly when encased in a thick and shiny layer of heavy parchment as a protective cover. This resemblance gave rise to the alternative name of pipe rolls, used in Latin as *pipa* from the mid-twelfth century, and in English as 'pipes' from the mid-fifteenth century.

As to their importance, pipe rolls were the record of the central government's financial relationship with its officials, in the counties and in other organs of the administration, as well as with individuals who owed money to the state. The rolls were intended for preservation and reference, and notes added to the rolls in later years demonstrate that they were consulted decades after they were compiled. The audit process by which they were produced involved examining the details of officials' accounts and attempting to confirm that they had delivered the cash they collected. It was both a way of ensuring that revenues were not lost, and a means of ensuring central control and officers' accountability.

How to begin

Faced with an actual pipe roll, or a set of photos of a pipe roll, it is hard to know where to begin. Perhaps the best approach is to practice first with an example of a roll where somebody else has already done the hard work. Comparing photos of a passage with an existing transcript should help to make you familiar with the forms of the letters used, and the way in which words are abbreviated. Here is some sound advice from Johnson and Jenkinson of the Public Record Office, more than a hundred years ago:

> The beginner will be well advised to attempt at first only documents of which he [sic] can without difficulty obtain a correct version to compare with his own . . . .. The trained reader relies far more on knowledge of the document which he transcribes than on his palaeographical attainments. . ... It will also be found that the very possibility of seeing what is actually written often depends on the power of the reader to imagine for himself what ought to have been written, and to check his hypotheses by what he can see; indeed, it is not too much to say that you cannot read a word with certainty unless you know what it is.[1]

It is certainly true that knowledge of the likely contents of a document is a very good start. In the case of pipe rolls, we know in advance that they are about money, rather than, say, poetry or theology, so we know what sort of topics, and what sort of vocabulary, we are likely to find. It is also true that words in the roll may not appear to make sense unless you already know what they say, or are likely to say. Here, the predictability of pipe rolls is a great help. The same words keep recurring, in much the same combinations, so that a little practice will provide familiarity with the most common types of content. And in particular, it is worth noting the advice about starting with a document which has already been transcribed. This provides an initial guide to the conventions one is likely to meet, and allows the beginner to compare their own guesses with the readings provided by a more experienced transcriber.

Unfortunately, most of the available transcriptions of pipe rolls, as published by the Pipe Roll Society, can only be compared with the originals by visiting The National Archives and ordering up the actual documents. This is not feasible for most readers. Johnson and Jenkinson provided black-and-white plates of extracts from pipe rolls, which could be compared with their transcriptions and commentaries, in which they pointed out the characteristics of the hand used.[2] We have an even better resource: colour photographs of the complete pipe rolls from 1225 onwards are now freely available online. They may even be preferable to the originals for some purposes, because they can be blown up to larger than life-size, adjusted to improve contrast, and so on. Transcriptions of a few of these rolls have been published and could provide a place to start. Perhaps the best example would be the 1226 pipe roll; this is available in print, in a reliable modern transcription, and there is also a full set of photographs online.³ Similarly, short extracts from the 1237 and 1293 rolls are in Appendix 1, with details of the corresponding online photos. Comparing these extracts with the photos should help the beginner to see examples of many of the forms of abbreviation and the accounting conventions which recur throughout the pipe rolls.

Language

The pipe rolls are all written in Latin, but it is mostly a very simple Latin, a long way from the classical Latin that was once taught at school. You seldom need to worry about subjunctives and conditional clauses, or to hunt for verbs hidden at the very end of tortuous sentences. Much of the text is written in straightforward, present-tense Latin, using the sentence structure with which the clerks were familiar from English or French: subject-verb-object, rather than the classical subject-object-verb. A single verb, like *debet*, may be used to begin a long list of verbless entries, sometimes introduced by *Et*. The pipe rolls also use a Latin vocabulary that has moved quite a long way from classical Latin, so that a specifically medieval Latin dictionary may be necessary to look up unfamiliar words.⁴ Spelling too changed from classical norms, with *nichil* in place of *nihil*, for instance, and the *ae* ending of many nouns reduced to *e* – in our 1237 example, we find *Sancte*, *filie*, and *aule*.

Some common words recur, sometimes with new forms or meanings. For example, the word *idem* is used frequently to refer to a person previously mentioned, particularly in the phrase *Idem vicecomes* (often abbreviated to *Id' vic'*), to introduce an entry concerning the sheriff of the county; in the plural, at the beginning of a sentence, it is written *iIdem*, with the capital as the second letter. One of the most common words is *de*, with a much wider range of meanings than in classical Latin, perhaps influenced by French. It is of course used in personal names, referring to both French and English places: in our 1237 example in Appendix 1, Walter *de Verdon'* and John *de Tywe*. But it is also used more generally to mean *of* or *from*: again from 1237, the abbot *de Oseneye*, the monks *de Thame*. The prevalence of *de* as an all-purpose preposition means that it appears 27 times in about 480 words of that example.

Both English and French influenced the clerks' vocabulary, when there was no Latin word available, or they did not know one. A couple of examples from the 1259 pipe roll: *Johannes Knyt tethingman de Mucheldevr'* does not even try to find the Latin word for the head of the tithing, or to give it a Latin case ending; *j bonum chaszur* and *x chaszurs* not only use a French word for a type of horse (a hunter) but also use the French plural.

The clerks were also quite casual about their Latin grammar. Within a few lines, one might find the plural of *feodum* as both *feodi* and *feoda*; *in rotulo sequente* and *in rotulo sequenti*. Of course, contracting words had the incidental advantage that it was no longer necessary to show the case ending, particularly for proper nouns.

Abbreviations

Any photograph of a pipe roll will show that many words are abbreviated and that there is a wide variety of abbreviations to be found throughout the rolls. To take a sample from the 1297 pipe roll extract in Appendix 1, first as it appears in the original, then showing an expanded version, filling out the abbreviations in italics, and removing the stops which the original places before and after numbers:[5]

Id' vic'. deb'. xviij. d'. de. iij. forg' in Oxon'. Et. viij. d'. de p'prestur'. Et. viij. d'. de Rob'to. le M'cer. S'm^a. ij. s'. x. d'. d' quib's. ball'. ville Oxon'. resp'. i'. Ite'. Berk'

Id*em* vic*ecomes* deb*et* xviij d. de iij forg*iis* in Oxon'. Et viij d. de p*ur*prestur*is*. Et viij d. de Rob*er*to le M*er*cer. S*umma* ij s. x d. *de* quib*us* ball*ivus* ville Oxon' resp*ondet in* Ite*m* Berk'.

This is a fairly typical example of the degree of abbreviation to be found (and it does not bother to expand the conventional abbreviations for money, or the place-names). Although it may appear intimidating, it is worth noting that many of the abbreviated words are the common elements which are likely to recur throughout the rolls, particularly the words concerned with accounting. The clerks who wrote the rolls were naturally concerned to save themselves time and effort. At the extreme, they would write just a few initials for recurring phrases: a debt of one mark for the sale of wine against the assize would be recorded in full as *j marca pro vino vendito*; the clerk wrote only *.j. m' p' v' v'*.[6] The clerks knew that the rolls were not intended to be read by outsiders, unfamiliar with their conventions; they were for reference within the Exchequer, where knowledge of these abbreviations could be taken for granted.

For the most part, the abbreviations in pipe rolls use a few conventional signs to indicate omitted letters. Some are specific, replacing a particular group of letters with an abbreviation sign: *p* for *per*, either as the word itself, or as a syllable in a longer word, for example. Others are just general-purpose indicators of omissions, particularly the dash above the last or only letter in a word, showing that the remainder of the word has been left out. (This dash can also be used over a vowel, to indicate that a following *m* or *n* has been omitted.) There are also instances of entire words being replaced by symbols, known as Tironian notes, resembling 7 or ꝯ for *et*, and ÷ for *est*. There are far too many possible abbreviations to include in a work like this; a full list can be found in useful guides such as *The Record Interpreter* (where the section on Latin abbreviations occupies 163 pages, explaining why such a list is not attempted here).[7]

Abbreviation is naturally carried furthest in the most common words and phrases. These were repeated so often that it was worth saving time when writing them; similarly, there would be little doubt about their meaning when they were read. The bulk of the pipe rolls, particularly the county accounts, is so repetitious that a few set phrases recur over and over. It is therefore worth noting some of these phrases, particularly those recording debts and payments, so that they can be recognized even when they are abbreviated. Similarly, the conventions of layout and terminology are not self-evident, but they are generally consistent and begin to make sense as the reader becomes familiar with them.

Headings

The long lists of entries in the county accounts are broken up by occasional headings, usually distinguished only by being centred on the membrane (rather than being larger or more ornate than the surrounding text). There are two headings to be found toward the end of every county account. The new entries added to the roll each year are grouped at the foot of the account, under the heading *Nova oblata* – literally, 'New offerings'. The entries which were new in the previous year, and are still outstanding, appear just above the current year's *Nova oblata*, under the heading *De oblatis* – 'Of offerings'.

Groups of new debts related to a particular court, such as the judicial eyres which travelled around the counties to hear cases, were often added to the rolls under a heading such as *De placitis foreste per* [name of judge] or *De amerciamentis per* [name of judge]. The same was true for debts owed for a particular tax, with a heading like *Scutagium Wallie*, for the scutage raised for a campaign in Wales. Any outstanding debts, together with their headings, were then copied into the following year's roll, with newer debts appearing beneath them. In this way, the debts, and their headings, gradually made their way toward the beginning of the county's entries; old debts above were paid off or pardoned, and disappeared from the rolls, while newer debts were added below. These headings are useful for finding individual entries, if one is tracing a debt from one year to the next. The headings act as signposts, showing a particular debt's relative position within the county account.

Numbers

The pipe rolls use only Roman numerals. 'Arabic' numerals were known at this time, but not used by the Exchequer. There are a few differences worth noting between the normal Exchequer style and classical Latin usage.

The number one is normally written as *j* rather than *i*, and j is also used to end the numbers ij, iij, and iiij. The same is true when these numbers up to four are combined with larger numbers, such as vij, Lxij, and so on. The numbers j, v, and x are generally written as lowercase letters, whether alone or when combined in numbers like xxvij. Larger numbers, L, C, D, and M, are found in both uppercase and lowercase forms. The use of the lowercase l for 50 can cause confusion when £51 is written as *lj li'*. It is worth noting that iiij is used rather than iv, but that 9 is ix and 40 is xl or xL (the subtractive forms). On the other hand, the subtractive forms for 400 and 900 (CD and CM) are not usually found, but CCCC and DCCCC instead.

The number 80 is written as iiij with xx above it – that is, four-score. Rather as in French today, numbers from 81 to 99 are written by combining iiij^{xx} with the numbers from j to xix. This means that 90 is iiij^{xx} x, rather than the subtractive form xC. (Very occasionally, 120 is written as six-score, vj^{xx}, the old 'long hundred'.) Numbers are often separated from the surrounding text by stops placed before and after them. Long numbers, combining several elements, might be written with stops both around them and within them, separating their components, such as .c.iiij^{xx}.xvij. for 197. Similarly, long numbers are sometimes written using the Tironian *et* symbol: .CC 7 xvj. for 216.

The Exchequer clerks occasionally had to deal with large numbers, and when they did they often resorted to combining words and numerals. Amounts in the thousands may be written simply as .M.M.M. for 3,000, but quite often abbreviated words are used: .M^l.M^l.M^l. for 3,000, or .v^{que}.mill'. for 5,000. One can find quite elaborate combinations of forms used to express large numbers: for instance, .xv.mill' 7 xLiij. for 15,043, and .M^l 7 Dc 7 xxvij. for 1,627.[8]

Smaller numbers are also sometimes written as a combination of the numeral and the written form of the word. This can happen with cardinal numbers, such as iiij^{or} for 4, and v^{que} for 5; the appropriate case ending sometimes appears in phrases such as *de prestito ij^{orum} equorum*, or *de iij^{bus} annis preteritis*. It also happens with fractions and ordinal numbers, in instances such as the divisions of a fee: *de iiij^{ta} parte j feodi*, or *de xxx^{ma} parte*. A fairly frequent instance is in references to other rolls, as *sicut continetur in rotulo xxiiij^{to}*; the combination of numeral and word can be taken further, with references to the 41st roll appearing as *in rotulo xlj^o* or *xlprimo*.

Money

The money of account used in the pipe rolls was much more complex than the actual cash used for transactions. For most of the thirteenth century, there was only one coin in use, the silver penny. Irish and Scottish pennies were minted to the same standards of weight and silver content as English coins, so that coins from all three countries were used interchangeably. Halfpennies and farthings were occasionally minted, but fractional amounts were usually handled by cutting pennies into halves or quarters. Large amounts had to be transported around as coins: when Henry III went to Gascony in 1253, the Exchequer sent him £8,700 in cash, which would have come to over two million pennies, weighing about three tonnes.[9]

Actual cash transactions were carried out using pennies, but the pipe rolls recorded them in terms of pounds, marks, shillings, and pence. These were almost invariably abbreviated as *li'*, *m'*, *s'*, and *d'*, respectively. The relationship of these nominal units was:

12 pence =		1 shilling
20 shillings =	240 pence =	1 pound
²/₃ pound =	160 pence =	1 mark

The mark, and fractions of a mark, were used fairly often in fines and amercements, for instance. They thus crop up in pipe roll entries, sometimes expressed as marks, half marks, and quarter marks, sometimes as their equivalents in shillings and pence (13*s*. 4*d*., 6*s*. 8*d*., and 3*s*. 4*d*., respectively). Half a mark was written as *dim' m'* or *di' m'*. Marks also occurred frequently in the regular payments known as fixed alms – each county's fixed alms included one mark a year for the Templars. The use of the mark complicates calculations, but the Exchequer clerks seem not to have found it a problem. They sometimes seem to have behaved as if there were two parallel systems of counting money, so that we find some figures in pounds, shilling, and pence, together with conversions into marks, shillings, and pence: the 1258 memoranda roll, for example, shows the total amount paid in at Easter in two forms, first as £1,295 7*s*., then as 1,943*m*. 4*d*.[10] This is an accurate conversion, but it is hard to see its utility. For our purposes, and mental arithmetic, it usually suffices to remember that three marks equal two pounds.

Fractions of a penny are shown as: *ob'*, for *obolus*, a halfpenny; and *q^a'*, for *quadrans*, a farthing or quarter-penny. These are written after the number of pence, as *iij d' ob'*, rather than together with the pence, 3½*d*., as we would do.

Particularly in the 1250s, when Henry III was accumulating a stockpile of gold, the pipe rolls include references to debts expressed in pounds or marks of gold. These were usually fines which had been denominated in gold and were originally intended to be paid into the Wardrobe rather than the Exchequer, so that they would be controlled by Henry himself. Typically, they were fines such as one mark of gold to avoid having to incur the obligation to become a knight, or two marks of gold to have a charter giving the right to hold a market.[11] Such fines were sometimes actually paid in gold, but more often in silver coins, at a fixed exchange rate of ten silver marks for one gold mark. Henry could then use the silver to buy gold, which he intended to use for minting a new gold penny. This plan was a flop, and the accumulated treasure was soon spent, but the references to these fines add a little complexity to the pipe rolls. It generally suffices to multiply any references to marks or pounds of gold by ten, to arrive at the equivalent in the silver currency which was in normal use.

Blanching

The rolls contain numerous references to sums of money owed or paid *blanch* – this is usually shown as the abbreviation *bl'* following an amount. Such references occur most often in the fixed, recurring entries such as the county farms (as shown in the Oxfordshire example in Appendix 1). Originally, blanching referred to checking whether coins used for payment were of the correct quality, and increasing the number of coins paid to compensate for any deficiency in their silver content. By the thirteenth century, this was no longer so necessary, as recoinages ensured that coins were fairly consistent and reliable in their purity. The Exchequer, however, retained blanching as an accounting device: any amount shown as 'blanch' would have to be increased by one-twentieth to give the amount to be paid in actual coins. The 1237 example thus shows the net farm for Oxfordshire as £24 10*s*. 2*d*. blanch, amounting to £25 14*s*. 8*d*. by number. (One can check this by thinking of it as adding a shilling in the pound, for each full pound, plus *pro rata* amounts for shillings and pence; alternatively, just convert both sums to pence, and 5,882*d*. times 1.05 comes out as 6,176.1*d*.)

Blanching is thus a relic of previous practices, which the Exchequer may have retained out of inertia, rather than simply increasing the nominal amounts involved. Alternatively, it may have been kept because it provided the Exchequer with a slight financial advantage, when a sheriff's expenditure in cash was converted into a blanch sum before deduction from a blanch farm, and only then was the result converted into cash (rather than treating the entire transaction in cash terms): in our 1237 example, this procedure produced a gain for the Exchequer of about 6*s*.

Dates

Pipe rolls occasionally give the day and month in the form with which we are now familiar (and sometimes get that wrong – the 1259 pipe roll has a reference to the 39th day of January).[12] More often, they use an established set of saints' days, and other feasts such as Easter, to refer to days within a year. There was a list of such feast days in the *Black Book of the Exchequer*, which the Exchequer clerks used for reference.[13] For a given day, the clerks would not necessarily refer to the particular saint associated with that day but instead show the day of the week, plus a reference to a memorable feast day nearby. This meant referring to the eve or morrow of the feast (the days before and after), or the use of a construction like 'the Monday next after the feast of the Assumption of the Blessed Virgin'.

Years are almost always indicated by the regnal year (the year of the current king's reign). A simple reference to, say, the 10th year means the 10th year of the current reign. References to years from past reigns are indicated by a terse abbreviation, like *R.J.* or *R.H.* to show that this is a regnal year of king John or king Henry. Regnal years of course depended on the date on which a reign was considered to have begun. For the thirteenth century, fortunately, there are only three reigns to consider. Henry III's first regnal year began on 28 October 1216; Edward I's on 20 November 1272. If one can remember these dates, it is then a simple matter of mental arithmetic to work out when a given regnal year begins (although still easier to look it up). John, however, was (predictably) awkward, with a reign beginning on Ascension Day 1199, and each regnal year thereafter similarly starting from Ascension Day. Ascension Day is a movable feast, falling on variable dates in May or June each year. This makes dating particularly difficult: John's 16th year, for example, runs from 8 May 1214 to 27 May 1215, so that this regnal year includes dates like 12 May twice over. Because the Exchequer generally used regnal years in preference to calendar years, we are at least spared having to wonder whether they meant a year which began on 1 January or on some other date, such as Christmas or 25 March.

Some pipe roll accounts record transactions between specific dates, mixing feast days with ordinary calendar days. Wardrobe accounts in the reign of Henry III, for example, cover such periods as: 'from Wednesday before the feast of St. Dunstan, 18th year, to Saturday in the Invention of the Holy Cross, 20th year'; 'from Sunday next after the feast of St. Valentine, year 36, to the feast of the apostles Simon and Jude, beginning year 37'; and 'from Friday next after the feast of St. Peter ad Vincula, 49th year, to the third day of March, 52nd year'.[14] The only way to translate such dates into something meaningful is to start with a list of saints' days, which would show, for instance, that St. Peter ad Vincula is 1 August; then look up the 49th year of the reign, which was 1264–65; then use a calendar for 1265 to establish that the Friday after 1 August in that year fell on 7 August. Fortunately, this convoluted process can all be accomplished with a single book, *A Handbook of Dates*.[15]

Pipe roll years

For the sake of brevity and simplicity, this book refers to pipe rolls by the year in which they end: in other words, the first surviving roll, referred to as the 1130 pipe roll, is the one nominally covering the period from 30 September 1129 to 29 September 1130, inclusive.

The Exchequer used regnal years to indicate the year to which its own records belonged. The Exchequer's year always began on the morrow of Michaelmas – 30 September. Its records were drawn up so that each pipe roll or memoranda roll covered a year ending at Michaelmas, and each roll was referred to by the regnal year in which that Michaelmas fell, and the Exchequer year ended. The 1226 pipe roll, for instance, covers the year ending on 29 September 1226, and is headed *Annus decimus regis Henrici tercii* for the tenth year of Henry III's reign – the regnal year which ended on 27 October 1226, and thus included that Michaelmas. Obviously, that roll did not include the full regnal year, and did include the last month of the ninth year; this overlap was sometimes recognized by referring to a roll as being the roll of a certain year *beginning* (in this case, it would be year 10 beginning, because it is the period which includes the beginning of regnal year 10).[16]

The pipe rolls also refer back to entries in previous rolls with phrases like *in rotulo xviii* (when it is the current reign, in this case 18 Henry III, or 1233–34) or *in rotulo xiv R. J.* (the fourteenth year of king John). Regnal years are also often used in titles of publications. The 1226 roll, for instance, was published as *The Great Roll of the Pipe for the Tenth Year of the Reign of King Henry III: Michaelmas 1226*. This is not only long-winded but also confusing for those of us who have not memorized the dates on which each king's reign began. Much easier just to refer to the 1226 roll.

There is a further complication for pipe rolls from the early years of Henry III's reign. There was no pipe roll for 1217, during the civil war. The first pipe roll to be produced in his reign was that for 1218, which was his second regnal year. References within the pipe rolls of this period to the first roll of Henry III actually mean the first to be produced, rather than the roll of the first year. Similarly, the second roll might mean the roll of 3 Henry III, and so on.[17] This additional confusion is an additional reason for sticking to the simplicity of references like 'the 1218 pipe roll', meaning the roll for the year to Michaelmas 1218.

The rolls also refer to the four terms of the Exchequer year. These terms were similar to the terms of the law courts. They were: Michaelmas term, beginning on 30 September, the morrow of Michaelmas; Hilary term, beginning on 14 January, the morrow of St. Hilary's day; Easter term, beginning on the second Monday after Easter Day, known as the morrow of the close of Easter; and Trinity term, beginning on the day after Trinity Sunday. The last two relate to movable feasts, so the actual dates when these terms began would vary from year to year. The memoranda and receipt rolls show that there were vacation periods between the terms, recorded as *in medio tempore*, when it would seem that little was done.

Notes

1 Charles Johnson and Hilary Jenkinson, *English Court Hand A.D. 1066 to 1500: Illustrated Chiefly From the Public Records*, 2 vols. (Oxford: Clarendon Press, 1915), I, xxxvii–xxxviii.
2 For example, an extract from the 1256 pipe roll, transcribed in Johnson and Jenkinson, *English Court Hand*, I, 147–50. The corresponding photograph is vol. II, plate XVI. A modern colour photo of the same text is on the Anglo-American Legal Tradition [AALT] website: TNA: E 372/100 rot. 4 [image 8524]. References in this book to photos of pipe rolls and memoranda rolls on the AALT site, http://aalt.law.uh.edu/AALT.html, give the TNA catalogue number of the document, the number of the rotulet [rot.] or membrane [m.], and the number of the image.
3 Eric Gallagher and Lesley Boatwright, eds., *The Great Roll of the Pipe for the Tenth Year of the Reign of King Henry III, Michaelmas 1226*, New Series [NS] 64 (Woodbridge: Pipe Roll Society, 2022). The photos are on the AALT site: TNA: E 372/70 [images 6995–7118]. Some other possibilities would be the 1230 and 1242 pipe rolls, and the Surrey account from 1295: Mabel H. Mills, ed., *The Pipe Roll For 1295, Surrey Membrane*, Surrey Record Society (London: Wm.

Dawson & Sons, 1924, reprinted 1968). There is also the 1259 roll transcript in an unpublished thesis, available online (see Chapter 4).
4 The fullest and most relevant information is in Richard Ashdowne, D. R. Howlett, and Ronald Edward Latham, *Dictionary of Medieval Latin From British Sources*, 3 vols. (Oxford: Published for the British Academy by Oxford University Press, 2018). This builds on the earlier, and much shorter, Ronald Edward Latham, *Revised Medieval Latin Word-list From British and Irish Sources* (London: Published for the British Academy by Oxford University Press, 1980).
5 TNA: E 372/138 rot. 3 [image 1954].
6 TNA: E 372/103 rot. 1 [image 1659].
7 Charles Trice Martin, *The Record Interpreter: A Collection of Abbreviations, Latin Words and Names Used in English Historical Manuscripts and Records*, 2nd ed. (London: Stevens and Sons, 1910). Reprinted several times. The book is particularly useful because it is based specifically on the abbreviations to be found in English medieval records.
8 These are both in the Wardrobe accounts for 1265–68: TNA: E 372/115 rot. 1d [image 0971].
9 TNA: E 403/9 m. 1.
10 TNA: E 159/31 m. 24 [image 0076].
11 There is a long list of such fines in the 1258 fine roll: *Calendar of the Fine Rolls of the Reign of Henry III* [*CFR*; available online at https://finerollshenry3.org.uk/content/calendar/calendar.html] 1257–58, nos. 1182–1288.
12 TNA: E 372/103 rot. 6d [image 1776]. This bizarre date is also in the chancellor's roll, TNA: E 352/56.
13 Christopher Robert Cheney and Michael Jones, *A Handbook of Dates: for Students of British History*, revised ed., RHS Guides and Handbooks No. 4. (Cambridge: Cambridge University Press, 2000), 61. The *Black Book*, TNA: E 36/266, has not been published.
14 Benjamin Linley Wild, ed., *The Wardrobe Accounts of Henry III*, NS 58 (London: Pipe Roll Society, 2012), 1, 76, 130.
15 Cheney and Jones, *Handbook of Dates*. There are resources online for each of these elements of the date, but nothing, so far as I know, that makes the process as straightforward as using the *Handbook*.
16 Gallagher and Boatwright, *1226 Pipe Roll*, 1. Photo: TNA: E 372/70 rot. 1 [image 6997].
17 Reginald Allen Brown and James Clarke Holt, eds., *Pipe Roll 17 John and Praestita Roll 14–18 John*, NS 37 (London: Pipe Roll Society, 1964), 7–8.

2 The rolls system and background

Pipe rolls were part of a system of records which developed over time. This system was much more elaborate in the thirteenth century than it had been when pipe rolls emerged, early in the twelfth century. Much of the existing literature about pipe rolls concentrates on the twelfth century, influenced by the survival of the Dialogue of the Exchequer, written about 1180, but not necessarily applicable to later Exchequer practices. The publication of pipe rolls themselves has also concentrated on the twelfth century and early thirteenth century. The later rolls have to be consulted in person, or, more recently, online, to see how they came to differ from their predecessors.

Historical background

The origin of pipe rolls can only be a topic for futile speculation. The oldest surviving pipe roll is that for 1130, but that roll was not the first to be produced. The 1130 roll shows that the production of such rolls was already a going concern, and an extract from a roll of 1124 has been found. The next survivor is from 1156 (although there is a thirteenth-century summary of a pipe roll for 1155, which has since been lost).[1] From then on, there are rolls for almost every year until the production of pipe rolls was abandoned, in 1832. Their importance ensured that they were carefully preserved. In all, we still have 676 pipe rolls, held in The National Archives.

Over seven centuries, the role and contents of pipe rolls obviously evolved. The early rolls are largely concerned with sheriffs' accounts for their counties, and it is not until the 1220s that the rolls regularly contain the accounts of other officials, such as the keepers of the Wardrobe, the wardens of the exchanges, and the escheators who administered estates which had come into the king's hands. These accounts were known as foreign accounts ('foreign' in the sense that they were not the county accounts; nothing to do with being from overseas). They were increasingly collected together in a section at the end of each pipe roll, called the *Rotuli compotorum*. Another major change took place in the 1230s, when the manors and boroughs of the royal demesne were largely removed from the sheriffs' control, and administered separately. The demesne had originally been a major constituent of the county farm, the sum which sheriffs were expected to produce each year from their counties' revenues. From about 1240, many demesne properties were farmed out, with the sums due each year now appearing separately in the pipe rolls. The number of individual debts recorded in the pipe rolls also tended to increase, so that the rolls grew longer and longer. The 1130 roll contained sixteen rotulets; the next survivor, for 1156, had twelve rotulets, and in the mid-1220s the rolls still had only around fifteen rotulets. The number and size of the rotulets then expanded, reaching twenty-three rotulets by 1259 and fifty-six rotulets by 1301. This naturally led to repeated attempts to reduce the bulk of the rolls, by cutting out obsolete material, then by removing the county farms and the foreign accounts, which were put into a separate series of rolls. These measures, considered in more detail in Chapter 5, changed the character of the fourteenth-century pipe rolls (although they were still very large).

The pipe rolls of the thirteenth century are thus rather different from those which were produced before and after. They have received much less attention than the earlier rolls. Both the publication of pipe rolls and commentary on pipe rolls have tended to concentrate on the twelfth century. The thirteenth-century pipe rolls were part of a more complex system of records than their predecessors and have to be seen in the context of a developing bureaucracy.

The rolls system

Pipe rolls did not stand alone. They were part of a system of records, involving several other series of rolls used for storing information and for conveying information between government departments. Each of these series might deserve a book of its own, but a brief summary may help to clarify the process by which pipe rolls were compiled. There is a fuller description of how this worked for a single year in Chapter 4.

The Exchequer itself produced a number of rolls beside the pipe rolls. The *receipt* and *issue* rolls recorded money received and paid out by the Treasury, the part of the Exchequer which handled and stored cash, and produced the wooden tallies used as acknowledgements of payment received. Exchequer *liberate* rolls copied the writs which the Exchequer received, ordering it to make payments or to give allowances to officials. The *memoranda* rolls recorded things worth remembering, as their name implies; all sorts of information were noted down as each year progressed, then gathered together to make the *communia* section of the memoranda rolls. The communia contained such things as the appointment of officials, arrangements for debts to be paid by instalments, acknowledgements of debt, and instructions to the sheriffs. The memoranda rolls also recorded the dates set for sheriffs to account (the *dies dati*), and the amounts which sheriffs and boroughs brought to the Exchequer after Michaelmas and Easter (the *adventus*). The Exchequer sent out *summonses* to the sheriffs, listing the debts which they were expected to collect. The process of producing the pipe rolls was reflected in the *compoti* section of the memoranda rolls, noting outstanding debts for each county, the actions to be taken to collect them, and the sheriff's status after his account had been audited. The Exchequer also received written evidence of financial activities from sheriffs and other officials, as part of the audit process. Much of this documentation has disappeared, but there are still surviving examples of sheriffs' *particulars of account*, showing the traditional sources of income from the counties, and the detailed accounts of officials like the wardens of the exchanges and the escheators who administered property for the king. These often provide fuller versions of their activities than the audited summaries in the pipe roll foreign accounts.

The Chancery was the government department handling royal correspondence. It kept its own series of *liberate* rolls, copying the writs which it sent out concerning payments. It also recorded the fines; these were offers of payment to the king in return for a concession, which might be a favour or a routine writ. These were noted in the *fine* rolls, and periodically copied onto *originalia* rolls, sent to the Exchequer. Similarly, the law courts maintained their own series of court rolls, recording details of the cases they heard. When they imposed financial penalties, known as amercements, these were copied into *estreats*, also sent to the Exchequer.

There was thus a flow of information into and out of the Exchequer, as well as a flow of cash. The Exchequer received originalia and estreats and then sorted the debts by county. It could add this to its own knowledge of outstanding debts, as recorded in the latest pipe roll, and draw up summonses for each county. The summonses were sent to the sheriffs, instructing them to collect the fines, amercements, and other debts outstanding from residents of their counties. The sheriffs delivered what they had collected, nominally at the *adventus* twice a year, and received tally sticks recording their payments. The cash they produced was recorded in the receipt rolls. The sheriffs were given dates for their accounts to be audited, as shown in the *dies dati* section of the memoranda. At the audit, they produced the tally sticks and other evidence of their activities, and the results were entered into the pipe roll.

Chancellor's rolls

While the pipe rolls were nominally produced for the treasurer, who headed the Exchequer, there was also a parallel series of rolls, produced for the chancellor. The chancellor's rolls are identical in size and layout to the pipe rolls, and to a large extent duplicate the information which the pipe rolls contain. There are 615 chancellor's rolls still extant, covering most years from 1162 to 1832. A few have been published, to make up deficiencies in the series of pipe rolls, but the chancellor's rolls have generally been considered less important than the pipe rolls. They were referred to as 'antigraphs', and may have been less carefully preserved in the past. It is also possible that rolls from the two series may sometimes have been jumbled up, and filed under the wrong heading.

The only notable difference in coverage between the two series of rolls is that the earlier chancellor's rolls include the schedules of combustion, notes attached to the rolls showing the losses recorded when coins were assayed. That apart, their contents are mostly very similar, but not identical. The published pipe rolls have been collated with the corresponding chancellor's rolls, where they survive, and they all show minor differences. Mostly, these are just variations in spelling or the addition or loss of a few words, but there are enough such differences to show that one roll was not copied from the other, nor were they both produced from a common source, such as dictation to two clerks at the same time. For example, names may be given in their French form in one roll, in Latin in the other: del Bois and de Bosco, de Belchamp and de Bello Campo. The payment of a debt may be recorded in one roll but not the other, and so on.[2] The reasons for these differences remain opaque, but many may derive from the two rolls' clerks working independently to produce each year's roll, by copying material from the preceding roll in their own series. Each one thus copied and replicated a separate set of errors and omissions.

Pipe rolls on parchment

The actual pipe rolls, and the duplicate chancellor's rolls, are all kept at The National Archives (TNA), in Kew, London. They are catalogued in classes E 372 and E 352, respectively. Anyone with a reader's ticket can order a roll from the online catalogue and have it delivered to the Maps and Large Documents Reading Room. (Older records, up to the reign of John, may only be available in a special secure reading room.) Readers will then find out for themselves just how awkward the rolls are to manoeuvre and navigate. They are too big to lay out flat, except on the large tables intended for maps, and have to be held down with weights to stop them rolling up again. As rotulets are up to 1500 mm long, their contents can only be brought near enough for close reading if the roll is kept partially rolled, which involves constant readjustment to move up and down a rotulet. The width of the rotulets means that each line of writing is uncomfortably long, making it easy to lose one's place when moving from one line to the next. Turning from the face to the dorse of a given rotulet can be a fraught and noisy process. Nevertheless, for those who have the opportunity, seeing and handling an actual roll is an invaluable experience. It is also perhaps not an experience to be repeated too often, given the alternative means of accessing pipe rolls described below. The chancellor's rolls are only available at Kew, as they have not been photographed.

The National Archives online catalogue includes helpful descriptions of the various classes of document. Fuller descriptions and historical notes are often to be found in the old typescript catalogue, shelved in the Reading Room itself.[3]

Pipe rolls in print

The first pipe roll to appear in print was, appropriately, the oldest surviving roll, the one for 1130. It was published in 1833 by the Record Commission, the body set up by Parliament in the early nineteenth century to organize and publish public records. In common with other Record Commission projects, the roll was printed as a transcription of the Latin text in record type, a special typeface which attempted to reproduce the abbreviations of the medieval manuscript. Even at the time the disadvantages of this course were apparent. The editor of this roll, Joseph Hunter, remarked in another of the Record Commission's publications:

> In common with most of the other publications issued by the Board, the copies of the Fines in this work are given in a form approaching to the fac-simile. The disadvantage of this plan is, that a work is, on a first view, repulsive, and is never read with the same facility and pleasure that it would be, were the contractions dilated, and the cyphers made to give way to the words plainly written, which it is well known to an editor that they represent.[4]

Record type is indeed repulsive, but it took a long time for it to give way to 'words plainly written'. Fortunately, Hunter's edition of the 1130 roll has been replaced by a modern version which provides both the Latin text (with expanded abbreviations) and a facing English translation. That volume also includes a full set of photos of the roll on a CD – a technology which is already becoming obsolete, while printed books and parchment rolls still remain usable.[5]

The Record Commission also published a transcription of the 1201 chancellor's roll in 1833. Transcriptions of the pipe rolls of 1156–8 and 1189 followed in 1844. These were all produced in record type. Nothing further appeared for forty years, until the Pipe Roll Society was established, with the initial objective of publishing the remaining rolls of Henry II's reign. Its first volume, for the 1159 roll, was published in 1884. The Society operated on a fairly small scale. It published only 350 copies of each of its early volumes, and with volume 11 (the 1167 pipe roll) this was reduced to a run of just 250 copies. The Society continued to use record type for its early volumes, which appeared in rapid succession, covering the rolls up to 1175. As the introduction to one of its later volumes noted, record type gave 'a specious appearance of fidelity to the original'.[6] It also assumed some expertise in palaeography. Record type was finally abandoned with the publication of the 1176 roll, which appeared in 1904. From then on, the Pipe Roll Society continued to publish editions of pipe rolls, and other sources, in extended Latin, with regularized capitalization and punctuation. Extending the abbreviations and following a set of conventions for capitals and punctuation makes the rolls much easier to read for those who know some Latin. The Society has so far produced a complete series of pipe rolls up to 1224, with outliers for 1226 and 1230, and has plans to publish the rolls for 1259 and 1225. The only other pipe roll to appear in print is that for 1242, published as an extended Latin transcription in much the same style as the Pipe Roll Society volumes.[7]

Some extracts from pipe rolls relating to particular counties have also been published, including a series of accounts for northern counties extending into the thirteenth century. These are mostly Latin transcriptions, with the early ones in record type. The Northumberland pipe rolls of the reign of Edward I were begun as Latin transcriptions, and continued as English calendars.[8] There is also the Surrey account for a single year, 1295, in both Latin and English translation.[9] Similarly, there are a few publications with extracts from pipe rolls about specific topics, particularly the Wardrobe and Ireland.[10]

Nearly all the publications mentioned so far are solely in Latin, the older ones in record type, the more recent with extended abbreviations. Even the indexes of Pipe Roll Society editions were in Latin until the 1960s, which was not perhaps the most accessible approach.[11] The exceptions are the facing translations in the modern edition of the 1130 roll, and the 1295 Surrey account. There is hardly anything else translated into English, just three brief county accounts from the twelfth century, in the *English Historical Documents* series. This situation could have been very different if a proposed calendar of pipe rolls had been pursued. This was first suggested in 1926, and in the late 1940s, the Public Record Office, the predecessor to The National Archives, drew up an elaborate plan for publishing a calendar of the pipe rolls of Henry III's reign. This would have eliminated all the repetitive material which did not change from one year to the next. Rather than the painstaking transcription of entire rolls, the calendar would have concentrated on making available the important information from a series of rolls. Such a calendar would have allowed a much faster publication schedule and easier access to the significant material from the rolls, but the idea disappeared without trace, except for a series of calendars of Northumberland pipe rolls from Edward I's reign.[12]

Pipe rolls online

The continuous series of pipe rolls in print has only reached 1224, but photos of pipe rolls from that point onwards are available online. The Anglo-American Legal Tradition website contains several million images of medieval and early modern records.[13] These include the pipe rolls from 1225 to (at the time of writing) 1642. This vast project can initially seem daunting, but with a little application and practice it is possible to find your way around. The records are divided by reigns, so for the thirteenth century, after 1225, there are only two we need to worry about. The pages listing the records for the reigns of Henry III and Edward I each contain a column listing the pipe rolls, identified by their TNA catalogue number and by reference to the dates and regnal years in the leftmost column. For each roll, there are two ways to access the relevant photo. To go to a particular rotulet, click on the roll's number following E 372. That leads to pages of thumbnails for front and dorse, with markers to indicate where each rotulet begins. Alternatively, go to that roll's table of contents (shown as 'ToC'), to find a list of the counties and other accounts in the roll, with links to the relevant images. Finding a particular entry in the roll can still be a laborious process, particularly as the rolls become longer; some rolls from late in the century require more than two hundred images. Nevertheless, the site is an invaluable resource, which has made pipe rolls accessible to anyone with an internet connection (and the ability to read the rolls in their original form).

Another online resource is a series of digitized versions of the earlier printed pipe rolls, from the Record Commission and Pipe Roll Society editions. There is a useful set of links to more than thirty rolls available, on the 'Some Notes on Medieval English Genealogy' website.[14] There is only one thirteenth-century roll listed, the one for 1242. In addition, there is a transcription of the 1259 pipe roll in a thesis available online, as described in Chapter 4.

Dialogue of the Exchequer

Publications about pipe rolls, rather than pipe rolls themselves, begin with a text written in the late 1170s by Richard fitz Nigel, treasurer and bishop of London. This text, now usually known as the Dialogue of the Exchequer, first appeared in print in 1711. There have been several editions, under several titles, since then. It was originally published in Latin only, but the more recent editions include a facing English translation.[15]

Fitz Nigel was an experienced Exchequer official, from a dynasty of such officials, so his point of view was very much that of a senior insider. He was naturally keen to stress the importance of the Exchequer's role and to defend its way of working, even if it sometimes seemed illogical. He admitted that he was not familiar with some of the more menial tasks of the Exchequer, such as the assaying process, and had relatively little to say about the Lower Exchequer, which handled the receipt and payment of cash. Instead, he concentrated on the work of the Upper Exchequer, which set policy and carried out the audits of officials' accounts. Even here, his version of events is sometimes contradicted by the evidence of the pipe rolls themselves. The rolls do not actually follow the rules laid down in the Dialogue for their layout and phrasing, or its prohibition on erasing entries.[16] It is also clear that, despite what fitz Nigel claimed, the rolls were not written out in full during the audit process, as dictated to the clerks by the treasurer. Still less was it the case that the pipe rolls and the chancellor's rolls were identical, contrary to the Dialogue's account of one clerk copying exactly what the other wrote. Instead, much was written out in advance, copied from the previous year's roll, leaving blanks to be filled in as the audit progressed. Furthermore, if the Dialogue does not give a full or accurate depiction of the rolls in the twelfth century, it is still less reliable as a guide to the thirteenth century. It does not mention foreign accounts, or the use of lump-sum payments to avoid having to record numerous individual debts. It is largely concerned with the sheriffs' accounts for their farms, which became relatively less important as the demesne was farmed out. When fitz Nigel wrote, the rolls did not actually show the amount of the county farm for which sheriffs were expected to account; a later Exchequer official offered the bizarre explanation that this was to prevent sheriffs knowing how much they were expected to pay.[17] By the end of the twelfth century, the amount of the farm was the first item in every county's account, neatly demonstrating how quickly the Dialogue became out-of-date.

The Dialogue gives a top-down view of the Exchequer's activities, disregarding or ignorant of much of the detail of the pipe rolls. The first half concentrates on the Exchequer's personnel and their privileges, the second on sources of revenue and the mechanisms for collecting and auditing that revenue. It is of course extraordinary that a source like the Dialogue should survive, but it was not intended as an office manual for Exchequer clerks, and cannot be treated as a reliable guide to Exchequer procedure in the thirteenth century. It has been very influential, particularly in its comparison of the audit to a game of chess, played between the sheriff and the Exchequer officials, over the checked cloth on which calculations were made. These picturesque details recur in most accounts of Exchequer procedure, while little has been written about the actual workings of the Exchequer in the thirteenth century. The Exchequer was not static, and its procedures and even its language evolved as it established its identity.[18] The divergence between the Dialogue and the evidence of the later records was pointed out by Mabel Mills in her study of Exchequer reforms:

> Thus developments in exchequer procedure in the first forty years of the thirteenth century are important, because in these years were laid the foundations on which was erected the later exchequer system – it is in these years that it obviously diverged from the rules laid down in the *Dialogus*.[19]

Literature about pipe rolls

Seventeenth-century antiquarians were familiar with the pipe rolls and conscious of their importance. They transcribed extracts from the rolls, but the first significant account of the history of the Exchequer to appear in print was *The History and Antiquities of the Exchequer*, in 1711. This was written by Thomas Madox, another Exchequer insider: he had been a clerk in the lord treasurer's remembrancer's office and became historiographer royal. Although much had changed over the centuries, Madox was familiar with the archives, and he knew the procedures of the Exchequer at a time when pipe rolls were still being produced. His work, rambling and diffuse, is still useful as a collection of references to early rolls, showing examples of all aspects of the Exchequer's work. Indeed, his quotations from the rolls were so full and so wide-ranging that many later historians simply relied on his excerpts, rather than studying the rolls themselves.[20] Madox was in no doubt about the significance of the pipe rolls, of which he wrote:

> Amongst the Records of the Exchequer the *Great Roll* of the *Pipe* must be placed first, by reason of its pre-eminent Dignity. It was and is the most stately Record in the Exchequer, and the great Medium of Charge and Discharge, of Rents, Farms, and Debts due to the Crown. Into it the Accounts of the royal Revenue entered through divers Channels, as Rivers flow into the Ocean.[21]

Madox's *History* also included the first edition of the Dialogue, and an essay on the oldest surviving pipe roll. This includes an engraving showing the cupboards holding the early pipe rolls, as they were then stored in the Pipe Office, which is clear evidence that, even then, the pipe rolls were considered important, and in need of careful preservation. As Madox said, they were, next to Domesday Book, the most splendid records he had seen.

Further significant writing on the pipe rolls had to wait until the Record Commission and Pipe Roll Society had begun to produce editions of the early rolls. The existence of the Dialogue, and the fact that the rolls were mostly published in chronological order, meant that study of the rolls tended to concentrate on the twelfth century; the Pipe Roll Society's editions did not reach the 1200 roll until 1934. The Society's own *Introduction to the Study of the Pipe Rolls*, from 1884, is mostly taken up by a table of record type abbreviations, an explanation of the audit of the sheriff's account, and a glossary of Latin words and phrases used in pipe rolls. It would be useful for those studying the early rolls published in record type, but of little relevance for the thirteenth century. Similarly, R.L. Poole's classic work, *The Exchequer in the Twelfth Century*, was a pioneering exposition of the workings of the Exchequer, but limited as its title implies. It follows the Dialogue in treating the pipe rolls as primarily a record of the sheriff's debts, for the farm and other liabilities. On the other hand, Poole does note that the Dialogue deals 'perfunctorily' with a large part of the entries in the pipe rolls, the debts arising from judicial proceedings and taxation.[22]

Since Poole wrote, over a hundred years ago, there have been surprisingly few attempts to write general introductions to the pipe rolls and the Exchequer. The most notable are a brief booklet by David Crook, and two online guides, on the websites of The National Archives and the Pipe Roll Society.[23] There have been several studies of royal finance in the thirteenth century, particularly by Nick Barratt and Robert Stacey, which made great use of information from the pipe rolls, rather than writing about the rolls themselves.²⁴ On the other hand, few historians have followed Mabel Mills's work on the pipe rolls in the 1920s. She studied one year's pipe roll account for a single county, Surrey in 1295, in exhaustive detail: just fifteen pages of Latin text, with facing English translation, were accompanied by some seventy pages of introduction plus thirty pages of notes and index. She tracked the origins of the debts recorded in the roll, in some cases going back to 1166, or forwards as far as 1320, to find out what happened to outstanding debts. She also disentangled the process by which an individual's debts in several counties could be consolidated into a single sum. She showed how the sheriff's farm was made up, and related the payments of cash into the Treasury, as shown in the receipt rolls, to the payments recorded in the pipe roll. This had never before been attempted with such close attention and demonstrated that the pipe rolls could only be understood as part of a system of enrolment. They had to be read in conjunction with the Exchequer's memoranda and receipt rolls, and the records of other branches of government, such as the *liberate* rolls. She did this by going through the rolls themselves in the Public Record Office, the predecessor of The National Archives – very little of the material she needed was yet in print (which is still the case), so she had to plod through roll after roll to follow the thread of references to long-standing debts and, in some cases, their eventual payment. This is apparent from her footnotes: most of the references are to unpublished records in the Public Record Office. There was little previous work to guide her, so she had to work it out for herself.²⁵

Further studies by Mabel Mills drew attention to new procedures for the composition of the pipe rolls. These procedures were introduced in the first twenty years or so of Henry III's reign. Again, this was pioneering work, and some of her conclusions have since been questioned, but she was the one who spotted the significance of changes to the way pipe rolls were made up. She observed that in the twelfth century, the pipe rolls tended to record relatively few, relatively large debts, which were paid directly to the Treasury by the debtors. By the fourteenth century, there were large numbers of relatively small debts, paid as lump sums by the sheriffs on behalf of the debtors. This change 'from direct to indirect responsibility' meant that the Exchequer no longer had to produce tally sticks to acknowledge receipt of every debt, but could cut just one dividend tally for the sheriff, to cover the mass of individual debts included in the lump sum. The pipe rolls no longer had to record every single debt, because the details could be left on the estreats and originalia rolls, marked up with a *t* when a debt was paid in full.²⁶

Mabel Mills also saw the significance of the introduction of the profits required from sheriffs, over and above the county farm, particularly in the context of Magna Carta and the Exchequer's attempts to restore government finances in the early years of Henry III's reign. This was followed in the 1230s by the replacement of many sheriffs and the removal of the royal demesne manors from the sheriffs' supervision. She drew attention to the particulars of profit which the custodian sheriffs produced between 1236 and 1240. These showed the sources of revenue making up the county farm, without the demesne, and illuminate the processes behind the simple figures for county farm and profit which appear in the pipe rolls.[27] The demesne was kept in the king's hands for a few years, with royal administrators reporting on the revenues produced. The demesne manors were then farmed out, often to the manors' inhabitants. Some of Mills's conclusions about Exchequer reform in the 1230s have since been disproved, and much more is now known about the reform of the demesne, thanks to Robert Stacey.[28] Nevertheless, Mills remains one of the few historians who have studied the way in which thirteenth-century pipe rolls were compiled and used.

Another detailed study was produced by C.A.F. Meekings, who analysed the repeated efforts to cut the size of pipe rolls, by excluding repetitious and extraneous material. A more recent study showed how the Exchequer used pipe rolls to track debts over several decades, and sometimes even managed to collect debts long after they were incurred.[29] With those exceptions, the major contributions to knowledge about thirteenth-century pipe rolls have come from the introductions to the rolls published by the Pipe Roll Society (and thus of course refer mainly to the first quarter of the century, because those are the rolls which have been published). Many rolls were published with perfunctory introductions, or introductions which concentrated on pulling out the political or judicial plums from the rolls in question, but others added to knowledge about the way in which the rolls were produced. The editors could use examples from the rolls being edited, to show, for example, that: the outline of many accounts was written before the audit began, perhaps even before the Easter adventus; and rolls could cover events occurring after the end of the nominal year, up to the time of the audit.[30] Further information about the production of the rolls and their evolution over the course of the century should emerge as more rolls are edited and subjected to close scrutiny and correlation with other Exchequer records.

Notes

1 Judith A. Green, "'Praeclarum et Magnificum Antiquitatis Monumentum': The Earliest Surviving Pipe Roll," *Bulletin of the Institute of Historical Research* 55, 131 (2007). Mark Hagger, "A pipe roll for 25 Henry I," *EHR* 122, 495 (2007). Pipe roll for 1154–1155 in Hubert Hall, ed., *The Red Book of the Exchequer*, 3 vols., Rolls Series (London: HMSO, 1896), II, 648–58.
2 For example, the list of differences between the 1201 rolls in Record Commission, *Rotulus Cancellarii, vel antigraphum magni rotuli pipæ de tertio anno regni regis Johannis* (London: Record Commission, 1833), ix–xii.
3 The National Archives, "Discovery," https://discovery.nationalarchives.gov.uk.
4 Joseph Hunter, ed., *Magnum Rotulum Scaccarii vel Magnum Rotulum Pipae de anno tricesimo-primo regni Henrici primi* (London: Record Commission, 1833, reprinted by HMSO, 1929). Joseph Hunter, ed., *Fines, sive Pedes Finium: sive Finales Concordiae in Curia Domini Regis: ab anno septimo regni regis Ricardi I ad annum decimum sextum regis Johannis, A.D. 1195-A.D. 1214* (London: Record Commission, 1835), xxvi.
5 Judith A. Green, ed., *The Great Roll of the Pipe for the Thirty First Year of the Reign of King Henry I: Michaelmas 1130 (Pipe roll 1)*, NS 57 (London: Pipe Roll Society, 2012).

26 The rolls system and background

6 Charles Johnson, "Introduction," In *The Great Roll of the Pipe for the Second Year of the Reign of King Richard the First, Michaelmas 1190*, edited by Doris Mary Stenton, NS 1 (London: Pipe Roll Society, 1925), xiii.
7 It would not be feasible to list here all the pipe rolls in print. The volumes produced by the Pipe Roll Society, 102 so far, are listed on their website: https://piperollsociety.co.uk/full-list-of-publications. The 1242 roll is Henry Lewin Cannon, ed., *The Great Roll of the Pipe for the Twenty-sixth Year of the Reign of King Henry the Third A.D. 1241–1242* (New Haven: Yale University Press, 1918).
8 Society of Antiquaries of Newcastle upon Tyne, *The Pipe-rolls, or Sheriff's Annual Accounts of the Revenues of the Crown for the Counties of Cumberland, Westmorland, and Durham, during the Reigns of Henry I, Richard I, and John* (Newcastle: Printed by T. and J. Hodgson, 1847). Francis H.M. Parker, ed., *The Pipe Rolls of Cumberland and Westmorland 1222–1260* (Kendal: Cumberland and Westmorland Antiquarian and Archaeological Society 1905). Record type transcripts of Northumberland accounts from pipe rolls 1130–1272: John Hodgson, *A History of Northumberland: In Three Parts* (Newcastle upon Tyne: Printed by Thomas & James Pigg, 1820–58), Part III, Vol. III. Transcripts were continued into the reign of Edward I by William Dickson, "The Pipe Roll of 1st, 2nd, and 3rd of Edward I, with Remarks thereon, in continuation of the series published by the Rev. John Hodgson," *Archaeologia Aeliana* 1, 4 (1855). This was also published separately, with the rolls up to 1284: William Dickson, *The Pipe Roll for the First, Second and Third Years of the Reign of Edward the First for the County of Northumberland* [includes reproduction of MS transcription of Northumberland pipe rolls for 4–12 Edward I] (Newcastle upon Tyne: George Bouchier Richardson, 1854). This was followed a century later by a translation of the 1285 roll for Northumberland in A.J. Lilburn, "The Pipe Rolls of Edward I," *Archaeologia Aeliana* 4, 32 (1954). There were further instalments in vol. 33 (1955), 163–75, vol. 34 (1956), 176–95, vol. 35 (1957), 144–62, vol. 36 (1958), 271–96, vol. 38 (1960), 179–91, vol. 39 (1961), 327–43, and vol. 41 (1963), 107–22, covering the Northumberland rolls from 1286 to 1298 as English calendars.
9 Mills, ed., *The Pipe Roll for 1295, Surrey Membrane*.
10 Wild, ed., *Wardrobe Accounts*. Henry Savage Sweetman, ed., *Calendar of Documents Relating to Ireland Preserved in Her Majesty's Public Record Office, London*, 5 vols. (London: Longman, 1875–1886).
11 The last examples are in Brown and Holt, eds., *Pipe Roll 17 John*: Index Nominum et Locorum, 109–43; Index Rerum, 145–53.
12 Gloucestershire 1130, Staffordshire 1186 and 1187, in David C. Douglas and George W. Greenaway, eds., *English Historical Documents. [Vol. 2], 1042–1189*, 2nd ed. (London: Eyre Methuen, 1981), 609–23. Mabel H. Mills, "Correspondence: The Pipe Rolls after Henry III's Accession," *History* 11, 42 (1926). Public Record Office, *Prospectus for the Publication of a Calendar of Pipe Rolls, Henry III* (London: HMSO, 1949). A.J. Lilburn, "The Pipe Rolls of Edward I – Part II," *Archaeologia Aeliana* 4, 33 (1955): 163.
13 Anglo-American Legal Tradition, http://aalt.law.uh.edu/index.htm.
14 "Some Notes on Medieval English Genealogy," including a list of pipe rolls online: www.medievalgenealogy.org.uk/sources/pipe.shtml.
15 First published as 'Antiquus Dialogus de Scaccario Gervasio de Tilbury vulgo adscriptus' as an appendix to Thomas Madox, *The History and Antiquities of the Exchequer of the Kings of England, in Two Periods*, 1st ed. (London: Printed by John Matthews, 1711). Latin with English translation, and a useful introduction, in Charles Johnson, ed., *Dialogus de Scaccario: The Course of the Exchequer by Richard, Son of Nigel* (London: Thomas Nelson & Sons, 1950). English version as 'Dialogue of the Exchequer' in Douglas and Greenaway, *English Historical Documents 1042–1189*, 523–609. Most recent edition, with a new translation:

Emilie Amt and S.D. Church, eds., *Richard fitz Nigel, Dialogus de Scaccario: The Dialogue of the Exchequer; Constitutio Domus Regis: Disposition of the King's Household* (Oxford: Clarendon Press, 2007).
16 Mark Hagger, "Theory and Practice in the Making of Twelfth-century Pipe Rolls," In *Records, Administration and Aristocratic Society in the Anglo-Norman Realm*, edited by Nicholas Vincent (Woodbridge: Boydell Press, 2009). Ulla Kypta, "How to be an Exchequer Clerk in the Twelfth Century: What the Dialogue of the Exchequer is Really about," *History* 103 (2018).
17 Hall, *Red Book of the Exchequer*, II, 659.
18 Ulla Kypta, "The Way a Language Changes: How Historical Semantics Helps us to Understand the Emergence of the English Exchequer," *Contributions to the History of Concepts* 10, 2 (2015).
19 Mabel H. Mills, "Experiments in Exchequer Procedure (1200–1232)," *TRHS* 8, Fourth Series (1925): 169–70.
20 Madox, *History and Antiquities*, 1st ed.; Doris Mary Stenton, "The Pipe Rolls and the Historians, 1600–1883," *Cambridge Historical Journal* 10, 3 (1952): 282.
21 Thomas Madox, *The History and Antiquities of the Exchequer of the Kings of England, in Two Periods*, 2nd ed., 2 vols. (London: Printed for William Owen and Benjamin White, 1769), II, 112. Italics and capitals Madox's. The second edition of this work is more useful, as it has an index.
22 Pipe Roll Society, *Introduction to the Study of the Pipe Rolls*. Reginald L. Poole, *The Exchequer in the Twelfth Century* (Oxford: Clarendon Press, 1912), 168.
23 David Crook, *Pipe Rolls*, Short Guides to Records No. 39, (London: Historical Association, 1994). The National Archives, "Medieval financial records: pipe rolls 1130-c. 1300," www.nationalarchives.gov.uk/help-with-your-research/research-guides/medieval-financial-records-pipe-rolls-1130-1300/. Pipe Roll Society, "An Introduction to Pipe Rolls," https://piperollsociety.co.uk/contents-and-use.
24 For example: Nick Barratt, "Finance on a Shoestring: The Exchequer in the Thirteenth Century," In *English Government in the Thirteenth Century*, edited by Adrian Jobson (Woodbridge: Boydell Press, 2004). Nick Barratt, "The Impact of the Loss of Normandy on the English Exchequer: The Pipe Roll Evidence," In *Foundations of Medieval Scholarship: Records Edited in Honour of David Crook*, edited by Paul Brand and Sean Cunningham (York: Borthwick Institute, 2008). Nick Barratt, "Crisis Management: Baronial Reform at the Exchequer," In *Baronial Reform and Revolution in England, 1258–1267*, edited by Adrian Jobson (Woodbridge: Boydell Press, 2016). William Mark Ormrod, "Royal Finance in Thirteenth-Century England," In *Thirteenth Century England V*, edited by Peter R. Coss and Simon D. Lloyd (Woodbridge: Boydell Press, 1995). Robert C. Stacey, *Politics, Policy, and Finance under Henry III, 1216–1245* (Oxford: Clarendon Press, 1987).
25 Mills, *Pipe roll for 1295, Surrey membrane*.
26 Mills, "Experiments," 152.
27 Mabel H. Mills, "The Reforms at the Exchequer (1232–1242)," *TRHS* 10, Fourth Series (1927).
28 Nicholas Vincent, *Peter des Roches: An Alien in English Politics, 1205–1238*, Cambridge Studies in Medieval Life and thought (Cambridge: Cambridge University Press, 1996), 343–8. Robert C. Stacey, "Agricultural Investment and the Management of the Royal Demesne Manors, 1236–1240," *Journal of Economic History* 46, 4 (1986).
29 Cecil Anthony Francis Meekings, "The Pipe Roll Order of 12 February 1270," In *Studies Presented to Sir Hilary Jenkinson*, edited by J. Conway Davies (London: Oxford University Press, 1957). Richard Cassidy, "Recorda Splendidissima: The Use of Pipe Rolls in the Thirteenth Century," *Historical Research* 85, 227 (2012).

30 Patricia M. Barnes, ed., *The Great Roll of the Pipe for the 16th Year of the Reign of King John: Michaelmas 1214*, NS 35 (London: Pipe Roll Society, 1962), xxii. B.E. Harris, ed., *The Great Roll of the Pipe for the Third Year of the Reign of King Henry III, Michaelmas 1219*, NS 42 (London: Pipe Roll Society, 1976), xii–xiii. B.E. Harris, ed., *The Great Roll of the Pipe for the Fourth Year of the Reign of King Henry III, Michaelmas 1220*, NS 47 (London: Pipe Roll Society, 1987), viii–ix.

3 Pipe roll contents

To a large extent, the pipe rolls are occupied by a few repetitive elements. The simplest building block is the statement that a debt is owed, and has or has not been paid. The reasons for these debts are many and varied, but a few types recur: the sheriffs' debts for the county farm and profit; the farm of demesne manors and boroughs; fines; judicial impositions; and taxes. There are also the more diverse debts of the officials who appear in the foreign accounts. All these components of the rolls provide a wide-ranging view of government finance, but it should be remembered that much was omitted, and that thirteenth-century governments did not share our assumptions about budgets and balancing the books.

Debts and payments

Much of the pipe rolls is occupied by entries following a simple pattern to record debts owed to the government, and what had been done about them:

> A person or persons [owes/accounts for] a certain amount. They have paid [part/all] [in cash/by expenditure as instructed]. [They now owe an amount/they are quit].

Such entries were often written out in advance, leaving gaps to be filled in at the time when accounts were audited. The first gap followed the name of the person concerned (or a collective body, such as the men of a manor or the burgesses of a town). It could be filled with *debet*, if the debt was still owed, or with the phrase *reddit compotum de*, if the debtor had taken steps to pay some or all of the debt. The latter phrase, often reduced to the bare minimum *r' c'p' de*, could be literally translated as 'renders account of', or more straightforwardly 'accounts for' the sum owed.

When the full sum of the debt had been paid in cash at the Exchequer, by the debtor or by the sheriff on their behalf, it was recorded as *In thesauro liberavit* (or *liberaverunt*), usually reduced to *In thes' lib'*, or something similar. This was followed, often after a gap, by *Et quietus est* (or the appropriate grammatical variations of case and number for women and for plural debtors). In other words, they have delivered it into the Treasury, and they are quit, meaning that they no longer owe anything, and the debt no longer has to be repeated in the pipe rolls. These phrases usually appear towards the right margin of the membrane, separated by a gap from the rest of the entry.

When only a part of the debt had been paid in cash, the set phrases were: *In thesauro* [an amount]. *Et debet* [the remainder]. If the debtor was making partial payments under an agreement for payment by regular instalments (known as attermination), the entry would end with a note near the right margin: *Per annum* [an amount].

The sheriff's account

Each county account (until 1284) begins with the sheriff's account for the farm. These entries follow a set pattern, which can initially seem like a confusing jumble of debt, payment, allowances, and expenditure. They run together actual cash transactions with purely nominal amounts recording sums which were no longer owed. Our 1237 example, in Appendix 1, illustrates the set of components likely to turn up in the entry for the county farm.

The sheriff accounts immediately after the heading showing the name of the county. The first entry follows the pattern:

> Name [sheriff/custodian] accounts for [an amount] for the farm of the county. Paid into the Treasury [an amount/nothing].

It begins with the name of the sheriff. He may be given his title as sheriff, almost always abbreviated to *vic'*, or described as custodian: *ut custos*. If the account covers more than one year, or there was a change of sheriff during the year, this is also spelled out. If the sheriff does not account in person (which he was normally expected to do), his name is followed by the name of his deputy, with the words *pro eo* to show that the deputy accounts on his behalf. The rest of the opening statement follows the pattern we have seen above for accounting for a sum and stating how much has been paid. It shows the gross amount of the county farm and the amount of cash which the sheriff had paid. (Note that in the 1237 account each amount is given as so much money *blanch*, meaning that it has to be increased by one-twentieth to give the equivalent amount in cash. This is explained in more detail in the section on money, above.)

From that point onwards, the calculation becomes more complicated. Generally, the next entry begins *Et in terris datis*. This introduces the list of *terre date* – literally, lands that have been given; properties which once contributed to the county farm, but have since been given away or leased out separately. The sums which they formerly contributed to the county farm are therefore deducted from the gross amount of the farm. Similarly, in most counties there is then a set of entries introduced by *Et in elemosinis constitutis*. These 'fixed alms' are the regular payments which have also to be deducted from the gross farm. These could be payments for religious or charitable purposes, or simply payments to recipients of royal favour, which recur every year. Following these fixed amounts, the sheriff then accounts for the variable sums which he has been instructed to spend during the year. The examples in Appendix 1 demonstrate the range of payments which might have to be found out of the farm, in response to royal orders. These could include payments for building works, the maintenance of chaplains,[1] and the upkeep of 'approvers' (convicted criminals turned informers, who were paid 1d. a day), or any of the miscellaneous tasks with which the sheriff was burdened.

After all this, the calculation of the net amount owed for the county farm can be completed. In our 1237 example, the sum is relatively simple (apart from the conversion to blanch amounts):

Gross farm		£326 13s. 5d. blanch
Deduct:		
Paid into the Treasury		£12 14s. 7d. blanch
Terre date		£174 blanch
Fixed alms	£112 2s. 9½d. by number =	£106 10s. 7½d. blanch
Expenditure	£9 7s. 4½d. by number =	£8 18s. ½d. blanch
The sheriff owes		£24 10s. 2d. blanch

We thus arrive at the same liability for the sheriff as the Exchequer clerks did, although they did the sums without our advantages of using Arabic numerals and a spreadsheet.

The calculation of the sheriff's account became much simpler after 1284. As our other example, from 1293, shows, the Exchequer eventually accepted that the *terre date* and fixed payments were static, like the county farm itself. An unchanging amount could thus be deducted from the gross farm to leave the *corpus* or 'body' of the county, which would be the same year after year. The calculation for Oxfordshire is recorded in a roll drawn up to record the county farms and deductions as they stood in 1283.[2] This shows that the gross farm was still £326 13s. 5d. blanch, and the *terre date* still £174 blanch. After the fixed deductions, the outcome was that the sheriff owed £61 15s. 1d. blanch as the remainder of the farm, or *corpus*. This figure could then be repeated year after year.

Farm, increment, and profit

So what was the county farm, and why did it occupy such a prominent position in the pipe rolls? As usual, the answer seems to involve the Exchequer's reluctance to abandon old habits.

The farm was originally the most significant single component of pipe roll revenue. It was the amount which a sheriff agreed to pay each year, in return for the right to exploit the king's traditional revenues from a county, or pair of counties. These revenues included the income from the manors and boroughs which made up the royal demesne, the proceeds of county courts and some hundred courts, and customary payments which varied from county to county. In the oldest surviving pipe roll, for 1130, the amount paid for that year's county farms was £6,343, out of a total for the year of £14,481.[3] Over the following century, the farm became a fixed sum, with unchanging nominal values assigned to the manors and boroughs which contributed to it. The relative importance of this fixed sum dwindled, but it still retained its place at the head of each county's account. By 1259, the revenue from that year's county farm was £1,210 out of £21,630 total revenue recorded in the pipe roll – less than 6 per cent.

The gross farm had declined relative to other sources of income, but the net farm actually due from the sheriffs had been cut further, because a large part of their original revenues had been taken away. Over the course of the twelfth and early thirteenth centuries, royal demesne manors and boroughs had gradually been removed from the sheriff's supervision, and either granted away or leased out. These changes were accommodated in the pipe rolls by listing them as *terre date*, lands that had been given. Their nominal values were deducted from the gross figure for the farm which the sheriff was expected to pay. The revenues from the tenants of such properties were often higher than the nominal values attributed to them in the pipe rolls, but they were now treated separately in the pipe roll accounts, and no longer contributed to the sheriff's farm. This process of removing the sheriffs' responsibility for royal properties was largely completed by reforms in the 1230s.

The importance of the fixed farm was also diminished by inflation. Rather than resetting the farm, the Exchequer introduced additional items which the sheriff had to pay. It introduced an annual increment for four sheriffs (£10 in Bedfordshire and Buckinghamshire, £100 in Norfolk and Suffolk, £40 in Warwickshire and Leicestershire, and £13 in Worcestershire). This too became a fixed sum, and remained the same year after year.

Sheriffs were then charged with delivering an additional sum, known as profit, to be found from the same traditional sources. This sum varied, and may sometimes have been subject to negotiation, but tended to rise, particularly in the 1240s and 1250s. In round figures, profits and increments came to about £1,700 in 1242, £2,500 in 1251, and £2,800 in 1257. Sheriffs were thus expected to produce increasing sums from the same sources. This meant particularly the income arising from county and hundred courts. They were forced to squeeze the counties harder, leading to the discontent which found expression in the period of reform after 1258. The custodian sheriffs (see below) of 1258–59 produced a much lower amount, £1,475, and the levels of profit required from farmer sheriffs in the following years were generally more reasonable.

Farmer and custodian sheriffs

In most years, the sheriff of a county was appointed as a farmer – that is, he or she had to produce a fixed sum, the farm for that county, at the end of the year. (Yes, 'he or she': there were a few women sheriffs in the thirteenth century. The most famous, Nicholaa de la Haye, sheriff of Lincolnshire in 1217, did not have to account, because there was no pipe roll for that year. Ela, countess of Salisbury, was sheriff of Wiltshire for several years, usually represented by deputies but appearing in person to account in the 1237 pipe roll.[4]) The farmer sheriffs had the incentive that they could keep any revenue they collected over and above the farm; on the other hand, if revenues fell short, they had to make up the difference. The same principle applied to increments and profits, when they were introduced to supplement the amount which sheriffs had to deliver.

The alternative to farmer sheriffs was the appointment of custodians, recorded in the pipe rolls with the words *ut custos* after the sheriff's name. Particularly in the 1230s and in the period of baronial reform, there were years when nearly all the sheriffs were custodians. They were appointed on the basis that they would simply deliver to the Exchequer all the revenue they collected, together with a statement setting out the sources of this revenue, known as particulars of account. In return, the sheriffs were to be paid a fixed sum for their service. This arrangement had the advantage for the Exchequer of showing how much revenue might reasonably be expected from each county, demonstrating whether the farm and profit had been set too high or too low; an appropriate figure could then be set when a farmer was next appointed. It has the incidental advantage for the historian of providing detailed evidence for sheriffs' revenue in the particulars. This detail is otherwise obscure, because farmers did not need to explain how much they had collected, or where it came from, so long as they met their targets. The particulars show that each county was different: all had the profits of justice from the county courts, and some had hundred courts in the sheriff's hand, but there was also a wide range of traditional revenues making up the farm, varying from county to county. Unfortunately, no particulars have yet been published in full.[5]

Manors and boroughs

Some of the properties making up the royal demesne were always outside the county farms and appeared separately in the pipe rolls. As early as the 1130 roll, the royal manors of Corsham, Harnham, and Tew were being farmed by their tenants, and towns like Colchester and Carlisle were farmed separately; in that year, the citizens of Lincoln purchased the right to pay the farm for their own city, outside the county farm.[6] As time went by, more and more of the constituents of the royal demesne were removed from the sheriffs' control, appearing in the pipe rolls as *terre date* as they were leased out separately. This process was effectively completed in the early 1240s, after a period in which the remaining demesne manors were taken away from the sheriffs to be managed directly by royal officials. The Exchequer thus established reasonable values for the manors, which were then farmed out, mostly to their inhabitants, described in the pipe rolls as the 'men of the manor'. The new farms were well above the nominal values which had been used in the county farms: Lugwardine,

Herefordshire, for example, appears in the *terre date* in 1242 with a value of £15, 'for which the men of the manor answer below'; and below, the men of Lugwardine answer for £42 for the farm of the manor.[7]

The royal demesne thus continued to contribute to pipe roll income after its removal from the county farm. It also continued to provide a means for the king to gratify his friends and relations. The manors farmed to their inhabitants in 1241 included Cosham, which was later granted to the king's brother earl Richard for his maintenance, and thus ceased to contribute to the Exchequer. Similarly, Dymock was farmed for £50 a year in 1241, then granted to Ela countess of Warwick in 1249 for £3 a year, then quit of any rent in 1257.[8] On a much larger scale, in 1254, Henry III granted lands intended to be worth £10,000 a year to his son lord Edward. This included Cheshire, Stamford, Grantham, Bristol, and much else, and all these sources of income disappeared from the pipe rolls while their revenues were being paid to Edward.

Despite these deductions, the manors and boroughs continued to produce a substantial contribution to pipe roll income, amounting to some £7,500 in 1259. All the revenues collected in the counties by the sheriffs, largely deriving from royal lands, reached some £13,000 or £14,000 in the 1280s, out of an estimated total of some £27,000.[9] They thus remained a significant component of royal income, whether inside or outside the county farm.

Amercements

Justice made a major contribution to royal income, from amercements (monetary penalties), and from the chattels of those who had fled or been hanged or exiled. The courts which feature most prominently in the pipe rolls are the eyres and the forest eyres. The eyres were courts which travelled from county to county, in which the king's justices were empowered to deal with all pleas, both civil and criminal. They were also intended to investigate abuses by local officials and encroachments on royal rights. In principle, the eyre visited each county every seven years or so, and then heard all the serious cases which had arisen since its last visit. The forest eyres similarly visited the extensive parts of the country which were designated as royal forest, to administer its special set of rules.

The amounts raised by the eyres were increased by the imposition of collective penalties, known as beaupleder fines, which were levied at the start of the court to cover any procedural errors which those attending might commit. These payments in advance to avoid further penalties, taken from communities collectively, appear in the pipe rolls as fines *ante judicium*. They were naturally resented. The resentment increased as these fines, together with the other financial demands of the eyres, were ratcheted upward. The eyres were seen as devices to raise cash as much as to dispense justice. The eyre of 1234–36 produced just over £10,000; that of 1252–58, about £18,000, as shown in the pipe rolls.[10]

Amercements from several other courts appear in the pipe rolls, including the Bench and some specialized courts dealing with exchange and market offences. Amercements from the county and hundred courts are not shown in the rolls. The sheriffs presided over the county courts, and the courts of many hundreds (sub-divisions of the counties). The revenues from these courts contributed to the amounts which the sheriffs were expected to produce as farm and profit. They, therefore, do not appear separately.

Fines and offerings

Fines in the pipe rolls are not fines in the modern sense of financial penalties for breaking the law (those were known as amercements). Rather, they are offers of payment in return for favours or concessions. Some were imposed by the courts, like the fines *ante judicium*, and were clearly compulsory. In these cases, it is hard to see a clear distinction between fines and amercements. Others were more definitely voluntary and were recorded by the Chancery in the fine rolls. They were then copied into the originalia rolls, which were sent to the Exchequer, so that it would know what fines it needed to collect. The details were then added to the pipe rolls, in the *Nova oblata* section at the end of each county's account, because these fines were literally 'new offerings'.

The fine rolls for the whole century are available in print or online.[11] They show the range of topics which fines could cover, from the purchase of judicial writs costing just half a mark, to offers for marriages and wardships running into thousands of pounds. An extreme example would be the offer, in 1241–42, by Joan the widow of Hugh Wake, of 9,000 marks for custody of her late husband's lands, the marriage of his heirs, and freedom to marry as she wished; this fine was then entered into the Yorkshire *Nova oblata* in the 1242 pipe roll, which showed that she was to pay this fine in instalments of 630 marks a year.[12] Such large amounts were more common in the reign of John, who imposed arbitrary fines to escape his rancour and recover his goodwill. In 1207–08, John was offered fines amounting to some £22,000; in 1256–57, by contrast, Henry III was offered only around £4,000.[13] This decline in royal income is reflected in the pipe rolls which recorded the fines imposed and the amounts actually paid.

Taxes

Thirteenth-century kings could not rely on a regular income from taxation. There were no equivalents to an income tax or property tax, levied routinely, year after year. Each tax was a separate event, and in many cases a special organization was set up to assess and collect that particular tax, accounting outside the normal pipe roll machinery. Even so, the sheriffs could still be required to collect the arrears of such taxes, long after they were first imposed. These debts continue to appear in the county accounts in the pipe rolls for many years: the 1226 pipe roll includes debts for a scutage imposed in 1196; debts from the thirtieth of 1237 are still to be found in the pipe rolls in the 1280s.[14] Individual taxes could raise very large sums – the thirteenth of 1207 (a tax on rents and movable property assessed at one shilling in the mark, which is roughly one-thirteenth) produced nearly £60,000, collected by the Exchequer of the Thirteenth – but they only happened occasionally. Particularly after Magna Carta, it was generally accepted that taxation needed parliamentary consent, which was often not forthcoming: between 1237 and 1258, Henry III asked for a direct tax at least ten times and was always refused. He, and other kings, therefore had recourse to forms of taxation which did not need parliamentary approval.[15] The taxes likely to be found in thirteenth-century pipe rolls are the various fractional taxes, tallages, carucages, scutages, and aids. The terminology in pipe rolls is not always precise, with almost any kind of tax sometimes referred to as a *donum* or *auxilium* (although there was very little that was voluntary about these 'gifts').[16]

Fractional taxes

The largest amounts were produced by fractional taxes, sometimes referred to as lay subsidies, assessed as a proportion of the value of movable property. They were also the taxes which aroused parliamentary opposition. After John's thirteenth of 1207, the next fractional taxes were the fifteenth of 1225, the fortieth of 1232, and the thirtieth of 1237. Henry III was then unable to gain consent for a further tax until 1269–70, when a twentieth was agreed, nominally to finance the crusade of lord Edward, Henry's son. Edward was initially more successful in obtaining consent for taxation, with a fifteenth in 1275, then a series of taxes to finance his campaigns. These became so frequent in the 1290s that he too met parliamentary opposition, and was forced to make concessions. Some rolls survive, listing the amounts imposed, which were drawn up for the initial collection of these taxes, separate from the pipe rolls.[17] The debts for fractional taxes which then appeared in the pipe rolls are usually identified simply by their particular fraction, either as a word, like *quintadecima*, or a number, like xxx^{ma}.

Tallage

Tallage was a levy imposed arbitrarily on the tenants of the manors and boroughs of the royal demesne. (This is distinct from tallages of the Jewish community, which were handled by a separate Exchequer of the Jews; these were not usually recorded in the pipe rolls, except for William of Axmouth's brief account in the 1261 pipe roll for the 1255 tallage of 2,000 marks imposed on the Jewish community.[18]) Tallages were frequent in the reigns of John and Henry III, but that of 1268 was the last in the century. The pipe rolls often give details of the amounts assessed, which sheriffs were expected to collect. Communities usually paid a lump sum, rather than individual assessments;

this transferred responsibility to local authorities to determine what individuals should pay, leading to accusations of exploitation of the poor by their wealthier neighbours who dominated local government. Such lump sums, generally convenient round numbers, may have been agreed after haggling between the assessors and the community's representatives.[19] Some tallages were imposed *per capita*, which was unpopular with communities and inconvenient for administrators: the *per capita* tallage of London in the 1228 pipe roll produced a list of 215 individuals, owing sums from £2 upwards, as well as the sums due from twenty-four aldermen, each responsible for collecting tallage in their wards of the city. Individual payments were still being made, and recorded in the pipe rolls, as late as 1267.[20]

Carucages

The carucage was a land tax, assessed as a sum per carucate (a variable measure of arable land) or per plough-team. Carucages were imposed in 1200, 1217, 1220, and 1224, but the tax then fell into disuse, as larger sums were raised by the fractional taxes on movables. As with the fractional taxes, the carucages were initially assessed and collected separately, with their own accounts, a few of which survive.[21] Some debts were then pursued by the sheriffs, and appear in pipe rolls of the early thirteenth century.

Scutages

Scutages appear frequently in the pipe rolls, often in considerable detail because collection was entrusted to the sheriffs rather than being handled by dedicated assessors. The basis of scutage was the relationship between the king and his tenants-in-chief, who held land directly from him. Their holdings were assessed as a specified number of knights' fees. As holdings were sub-divided, tenants became liable for fractions of a fee. In principle, the tenants-in-chief were supposed to provide military service for the king's campaigns, contributing one knight for each knight's fee (which would hardly be practicable for those who held just a fraction of a fee). In practice, this obligation was commuted to a cash payment of a fixed amount per knight's fee, or per shield (*scutum*, hence the name). In the thirteenth century, this amount settled down at three marks or £2 per fee.

John imposed frequent scutages, which Magna Carta of 1215 attempted to limit. From then on, scutages were generally associated with particular military campaigns, and identified in the pipe rolls by the name of that campaign: the 1226 pipe roll, for instance, includes references to scutages of Bedford, Bytham, Ireland, Montgomery, Poitou, Scotland, and Wales. The amounts due initially appeared in pipe rolls within the *Nova oblata*, often identified by a separate heading. Taking as an example the scutage related to Henry III's inconclusive campaign in Wales in 1257, the Devon account is in the 1259 pipe roll, under the heading: 'Scutage of Wales, the shield assessed at 40s.' The sheriff then accounts for 40s. from Richard Burdun for one fee, and 30s. from Hugh Peverel for three-quarters of a fee. There is then a long list of further debts, some large, like £32 from the abbot of Tavistock, with sixteen fees, some tiny, just 8*d*. for the sixtieth of a fee. Such lists in the pipe rolls are a helpful way of tracing land holdings. They also illustrate how subdivision made scutage increasingly complicated. Disputes between Edward I and his tenants-in-chief over the amounts due made it difficult to collect scutage, and it declined in significance.[22]

Aids

Aids were also associated with the obligations of tenants-in-chief, and imposed on the basis of the number of knights' fees they held. A lord traditionally had the right to require aid from his tenants for his ransom, for the marriage of his eldest daughter, and for the knighting of his eldest son. This right was also claimed by kings, and used three times in the reign of Henry III: an aid of 2 marks per fee, for the marriage of his sister Isabella (who was of course John's daughter) in 1235; an aid of 20s. per fee, for the marriage of Henry's daughter Margaret in 1245; and an aid of 40s. per fee, for the knighting of lord Edward in 1253. This last aid was actually used to help pay for Henry's campaign in Gascony in 1253. There were no further aids in the thirteenth century: Edward I imposed aids for the marriage of his daughter in 1302, and the knighting of his son in 1306.

The first aid had its own collectors, and apparently its own rolls; outstanding debts from that aid were later transferred to the pipe rolls, for the sheriffs to pursue. The debts for the other two aids of Henry III's reign appear in the pipe rolls, at first in the *Nova oblata* then recurring for many years. They are often distinguished from other debts by a specific heading, as in an example from the Berkshire account in the 1254 pipe roll. There is a group of debts for this aid at the end of the account, under the heading 'Aid (*Auxilium*) granted to the king for making his first-born son a knight, namely 40s. from each fee'. It begins with the sheriff accounting for 20s. from Martin of Peasemore for half a fee.[23]

Introducing the foreign accounts

The early pipe rolls, in the twelfth century, were largely dedicated to the accounts of the counties. They also contained occasional accounts for other officials, such as the keepers of vacant bishoprics. These accounts were relatively short, and scattered among other entries in the rolls. This approach continued until the early years of Henry III's reign, when a number of officials' accounts were gathered together in separate rolls. Some of these accounts from 1224 and 1225 may have been intended to be attached to a pipe roll, and are laid out on rotulets using the same size and layout as the pipe rolls. They became a distinct roll, the *Rotulus de diversis compotis*, which also includes accounts for the Wardrobe and for various taxes, such as the carucage of 1220 and the fifteenth of 1225.[24] The Exchequer was evidently experimenting with ways of incorporating these diverse accounts into its record system. The next move was in the 1225 pipe roll, which includes a final rotulet endorsed *Rotulus Maneriorum de Anno ix°*, with accounts of manors which were in the king's hands. The 1226 pipe roll has the first clear example of a section devoted to foreign accounts, as the last of its fifteen rotulets. This included accounts for such topics as works at Dover castle, various manors and the lands of the earl of Devon.[25]

From then on, most pipe rolls included one or more rotulets dedicated to foreign accounts, known as the *Rotuli compotorum*. These were often placed at the end of the rolls when the rotulets were gathered for sewing together. Over the course of the century, these sections of the rolls grew inexorably, as more accounts were included, and accounts grew more elaborate. By 1280, the foreign accounts took up the last twelve of the total thirty rotulets of the pipe roll; this included six rotulets of escheators' accounts, three rotulets of manorial accounts, and several smaller accounts, for the Wardrobe, castles, vacant bishoprics, and fines imposed on the Jewish community for coinage offences. There was still more growth to come, so that the 1300 pipe roll, with a total of forty rotulets, included nineteen rotulets of foreign accounts: of these, nine rotulets were devoted to the accounts presented by the executors of the former keeper of royal manors in Holderness for 1295–98; two rotulets for the wool customs at various ports; as well as several manors, silver mines in Devon, vacant priories, and so on.[26] The continuing growth of the foreign accounts eventually led to them becoming a separate series of rolls, but during the thirteenth century, most such accounts remained part of the pipe rolls.

The foreign accounts are not presented in the same way as the sheriffs' accounts. The sheriffs' accounts for farm and profit, at the beginning of each county account, record their liabilities and payments, nominally for a single year, with any outstanding balance being carried forward to the following year; individual debts thus get repeated year after year. In the foreign accounts, an official also reports how much he owes and how much he has paid, but this account appears only once. It often covers an irregular period, perhaps several years, and is not repeated the next year.

It is worth noting that the foreign accounts record the financial status of the individuals in charge of a particular area of activity. They do not record the corporate liability of, for example, the mints and exchanges; they record the personal liability of the wardens of the exchanges, and outstanding amounts are collected from them and, if necessary, their heirs. At the end of an account, if an official owes money, it is treated as a personal debt. If they remain in post, the debt might be carried forward to the next accounting period. Often, it is transferred to the appropriate county account, and pursued by the sheriff in the normal way. For example, Nicholas de Clere was appointed as keeper of the vacant bishopric of Exeter from 5 August to

11 October 1280. His account in the 1289 pipe roll (there was often a considerable lag in catching up with such accounts) shows that he owed £331 from the receipts of the bishopric; it also has a note, which must have been added later, that he accounted in Devon in the 1294 roll. And in that roll, it showed that he had paid £300 into the Treasury, and still owed £31. The debt would then appear in the Devon account year after year.[27] Similarly, Roger of Haverhill was warden of the Dublin exchange for the king in 1251–54, and accounted in the 1254 pipe roll. At the end of his period of office, he accounted for £535 net receipts. He had paid most of this to the treasurer of Ireland, but still owed 5s. 4d. A note added at the end of the account showed that he answered for this in London in the 1261 roll. And in that London account, at the end of the *Nova oblata*, there is Roger's 5s. 4d. debt, with a note referring back to the original foreign account. Clearly, the Exchequer might move slowly, but kept track of even quite trivial debts. This debt would then be repeated in the London account each year until it was collected or given up as uncollectable.[28]

What's in the foreign accounts?

The foreign accounts are, by definition, miscellaneous – they are everything that is *not* a county account. They cover most types of government activity which produced revenue, and some government activities more concerned with spending money, such as building works and the supply of the king's wine. The Public Record Office produced a list of the contents of the foreign accounts (and similar enrolled accounts), which is a helpful guide.[29] Unfortunately, it does not include the accounts for taxes and customs duties, but with the help of this guide, it is possible to track down the other thirteenth-century foreign accounts most likely to interest historians. These include: military expenditure, particularly the provision of castles and ship-building; the forests, including the accounts of the keepers of the forests north and south of the Trent, as well as some individual forest accounts, recording revenue from the sale of wood; the accounts of the treasurers of Ireland, from the 1280s onward; some accounts for Cheshire and Cornwall, which were at times treated as the king's own property and excluded from the county accounts; and accounts of building works, notably for Westminster Abbey, the Palace of Westminster, the Tower of London, and Edward I's castles in Wales. Some categories of foreign accounts may be worth more detailed description:

Royal household

Various aspects of royal household expenditure are recorded in the foreign accounts. The Wardrobe managed finance for the king's household, receiving cash from the Treasury and from other sources. It produced accounts to be audited by the Exchequer from the 1220s onwards, but there are gaps in the sequence, particularly under Henry III. In the 1250s, for example, the keepers of the Wardrobe did not account for several years; this was at a time when the king was trying to build up a supply of gold without Exchequer scrutiny. At times, Henry III simply pardoned his keepers from having to account. The supply of wines for the household was occasionally treated as a separate topic, with its own account. There were also accounts for the queen's wardrobe of both Eleanor of Provence and Eleanor of Castile, and a few accounts for the households of Edward I's children. As yet, only the accounts for the Wardrobe under Henry III have been published and analysed; these include both financial records and inventories of jewels.[30]

Mints and exchanges

The pipe rolls include the accounts of the wardens of the London and Canterbury exchanges in an almost continuous sequence from 1220 onwards. These were the exchanges where foreign merchants brought silver to be recoined into English pennies. Except during the periods of recoinage, these exchanges were the only significant sources of new coins, so that their records are a significant record of the monetization of the economy and the positive balance of trade – merchants had to bring silver to pay for the wool they exported, which evidently outweighed imports of wine and other foreign goods. The exchange accounts have been used to show how many coins were being produced and how much profit was produced for the king, as well as much technical detail about minting.[31] There are also occasional records of offences against coinage legislation.

Ecclesiastical vacancies

Kings claimed the right, when a bishop or abbot died, to take over the administration of the vacant bishopric or abbey, and to receive the revenues during the vacancy. This 'regalian right' was obviously an irregular and unpredictable source of income, but it could be very profitable. This was particularly true when a bishopric was left vacant for several years, as sometimes happened. The accounts of the keepers appointed to collect these revenues appeared in the foreign accounts, providing information both about an important source of royal income and about the resources of the bishoprics concerned. Margaret Howell gathered together and summarized the financial results shown in the enrolled accounts for vacant bishoprics. These demonstrate how lucrative this right could be: when the rich bishopric of Winchester was vacant, from 1238 to 1244, the net receipts were £17,600.[32] The king could also benefit from payments to avoid the appointment of keepers during vacancies, allowing the prior and convent of an abbey to retain their revenues in return for a fine.[33]

Property income

Thirteenth-century kings derived much of their income from land: some was the crown's own property, the royal demesne, and some had come into the king's hands through forfeiture or the exercise of his rights over tenants-in-chief. In particular, when a tenant-in-chief died, the king had the right to administer his or her property until the heir came of age. The heir then had to pay a relief to be allowed to take over the inheritance. While such lands were under royal control, they could be leased out, or granted to royal family and friends, in return for a fine or as a favour. They could also be administered directly, by administrators who were expected to account at the Exchequer, and thus appear in the foreign accounts. During the reign of Henry III, the office of escheator emerged, with responsibility for the administration of property.[34] There are entries in the foreign accounts both for individual manors and for the escheators, reporting on the finances of a number of estates. Some of these accounts go into great detail, providing valuable information about manorial administration, crop yields, and so on. Others, particularly those for the two escheators responsible for the counties north and south of the Trent, merely list the net receipts from a number of manors; the figures behind these entries were provided in detailed particulars, some of which survive as separate rolls.[35]

Customs

The customs on exports of wool, woolfells (sheepskins with the wool attached), and hides made a major contribution to government income in the reign of Edward I. The customs accounts appear in the pipe rolls from 1280 to 1304. The first such entry gives an example of the range of information provided and the financial significance of the customs: it shows the volumes exported and cash received from twelve English ports in 1279–80, producing a total of £8,109.[36] Later customs accounts appear in a separate series of rolls.[37]

What's *not* in the pipe rolls

Modern readers might expect the pipe rolls to provide a comprehensive view of government finance in the thirteenth century. At that time, however, the idea of a national budget would not have occurred to the Exchequer. There is little indication that anyone even attempted to work out how much revenue the king might expect, until late in the century.[38] As Mabel Mills wrote: 'The medieval exchequer officials had grave difficulties in estimating current revenue: it is doubtful indeed whether any treasurer before 1360 knew accurately the king's annual income.'[39]

The pipe rolls were not used to calculate profit either. The rolls of the Exchequer are similar to contemporary manorial accounts in some respects, and the Exchequer may well have influenced the records kept by large landowners. Manorial accounts used a system of charge and discharge accounting, balancing receipts and expenditure. This was not intended to calculate profit and loss, but to demonstrate the liability of the official presenting his accounts. This applied to the reeves and bailiffs of manors, just as it did to the sheriffs of counties and to the other officials whose accounts were audited by the Exchequer and included in the pipe rolls.[40]

The pipe rolls do not include attempts to calculate overall figures for debts and receipts. They present accounts for individual counties, with no totals, and no attempt to draw up a comprehensive view for the whole of England, and still less for the entire extent of the royal possessions. Indeed, they do not even cover some parts of England. Several counties were excluded from the pipe rolls at various times, such as Durham, which was administered by its bishop; Cornwall and Rutland, when they were in the hands of earl Richard of Cornwall; and Cheshire when it was assigned to lord Edward. Ireland had its own Exchequer, producing its own pipe rolls, and its treasurer's accounts did not appear in the English pipe rolls until the 1280s. Similarly, before the loss of Normandy in 1204, there was a series of Norman pipe rolls.

Some major sources of royal income stood outside the pipe roll system. There was a separate Exchequer of the Jews, which administered the tallages and other impositions on the Jewish community. Some taxes, such as the fifteenth of 1225 and the fortieth of 1232, were collected by officials who presented accounts specifically for those taxes. These accounts did not appear on the pipe rolls and are largely lost. After 1294, some customs duties, a major source of revenue, were also enrolled separately.

Another significant gap in the pipe rolls' coverage of royal revenue was caused by the autonomy of the Wardrobe. This institution managed the finances of the royal household, travelled with the king, and expanded in times of war to become the department which controlled military expenditure. It received cash from the Treasury, which was duly recorded in the Exchequer rolls, but also collected some cash directly. The Wardrobe controlled a large proportion of overall government expenditure, with between a quarter and a half of the king's annual cash income passing through the Wardrobe in the 1240s.[41] The keepers of the Wardrobe were generally expected to account at the Exchequer, with their audited accounts appearing in the pipe rolls, but they often accounted several years in arrears, and sometimes not at all.

Taking together all these exclusions from the pipe rolls, this means that there are considerable holes in our knowledge of the total picture for royal finance. We should not expect pipe rolls to work like modern accounts, or to provide information which they were not designed to deliver. The Exchequer intended them as a record of debts, both outstanding and collected, and a check on the integrity and performance of the officials who were responsible for collecting these debts and making local payments. Pipe rolls still contain a mass of information about finance, government, and people in the thirteenth century.

Notes

1 The chaplain at the well in Woodstock is a reference to the chapel at Everswell, in the park around the royal residence: R. Allen Brown, Howard Montagu Colvin, and Alan John Taylor, *The History of the King's Works: The Middle Ages*, 2 vols. (London: HMSO, 1963), II, 1014.

2. In pipe roll TNA: E 372/129 rot. 13d [image 3518].
3. Judith A. Green, *The Government of England Under Henry I*, 1st paperback ed. (Cambridge: Cambridge University Press, 1989), Table 1, 223.
4. Louise J. Wilkinson, "Women as Sheriffs in Early Thirteenth Century England," In *English Government in the Thirteenth Century*, edited by Adrian Jobson (Woodbridge: Boydell Press, The National Archives, 2004). The 1237 Wiltshire account: TNA: E 372/81 rot. 13d [image 4601]. Her appearance in person is confirmed by the 1238 memoranda roll: TNA: E 159/16 m. 19d [image 0103].
5. There are extracts from particulars concerning court revenues in William Alfred Morris, *The Early English County Court. An Historical Treatise With Illustrative Documents* (Berkeley: University of California Publications in History, 1926), 197–230.
6. Green, ed., 1130 *Pipe Roll*, xxv, xxvi.
7. Stacey, "Agricultural investment". TNA: E 372/86 rot. 8d [images 5075, 5077].
8. CFR 1240–41, no. 756. *Calendar of the Patent Rolls Preserved in the Public Record Office, Henry III*, 4 vols. (London: HMSO, 1906–1913), 1247–58, 42, 539.
9. Michael Prestwich, *War, Politics and Finance Under Edward I* (London: Faber and Faber, 1972), 178.
10. Cecil Anthony Francis Meekings, ed., *The 1235 Surrey Eyre*, (Guildford: Surrey Record Society, 1979), I, 135. 1250s figure from pipe rolls TNA: E 372/96–105. Another calculation estimated that revenue from the eyre of 1252–58 amounted to 3.7–9.8 per cent of total royal income: Jens Röhrkasten, "The general eyre and royal finance," table 4.1, in Travis R. Baker, ed., *Law and Society in Later Medieval England* (London: Routledge, 2018).
11. Thomas Duffus Hardy, ed., *Rotuli de Oblatis et Finibus in Turri Londinensi Asservati, tempore regis Johannis* (London: Record Commission. Printed by G. Eyre and A. Spottiswoode, 1835). "Henry III Fine Rolls Project," accessed 16.2.22, https://finerollshenry3.org.uk/home.html. *Calendar of the Fine Rolls, I, Edward I, 1272–1307* (London: HMSO, 1911). The last reference omits routine fines, such as payments for writs.
12. CFR 1241–42, no. 105. In the 1242 pipe roll, TNA: E 372/86 m. 2d [image 5055].
13. David Carpenter, *Magna Carta* (London: Penguin Classics, 2015), 458.
14. Gallagher and Boatwright, eds., 1226 *Pipe Roll*, 129, 242. TNA: E 372/127 rot. 4d [image 3038].
15. Maureen Jurkowski, C.L. Smith, and D. Crook, *Lay Taxes in England and Wales 1188–1688,* Public Record Office Handbook (Kew: PRO Publications, 1998), xvii–xxxi. John Robert Maddicott, *The Origins of the English Parliament, 924–1327* (Oxford: Oxford University Press, 2010), 173. The standard work on taxation is probably still Sydney Knox Mitchell, *Studies in Taxation under John and Henry III* (New Haven: Yale University Press, 1914).
16. Gerald Leslie Harriss, *King, Parliament, and Public Finance in Medieval England to 1369* (Oxford: Clarendon Press, 1975), 19.
17. A few have been published: some accounts for the the fifteenth and fortieth in Fred A. Cazel, ed., *Roll of Divers Accounts for the Early Years of the Reign of Henry III*, NS 44 (London: Pipe Roll Society, 1982), 54–73. Fred A. Cazel and Annarie P. Cazel, eds., *Rolls of the Fifteenth of the Ninth Year of the Reign of Henry III for Cambridgeshire, Lincolnshire and Wiltshire; and, Rolls of the Fortieth of the Seventeenth Year of the Reign of Henry III for Kent*, NS 45 (London: Pipe Roll Society, 1983).
18. TNA: E372/104 rot. 1 [image 1853].
19. See for instance the list of tallages in CFR 1248–49, no. 96
20. TNA: E 372/72 rot. 6, 6d [images 1444, 1508–10]; E 372/111 rot. 18d [image 9644].

21 Cazel, *Roll of Divers Accounts*, 16–25.
22 TNA: E 372/103 rot. 6d [image 1776]. Jurkowski, Smith, and Crook, *Lay Taxes*, xix–xxi.
23 TNA: E 372/98 rot. 30 [image 8247].
24 This roll, TNA: E 364/1, has been published in Cazel, *Roll of Divers Accounts*.
25 The 1225 roll: TNA: E 372/69 rot. 15, 15d [images 1245–8, 1303–5]. The 1226 roll: Gallagher and Boatwright, *1226 Pipe Roll*, 262–81.
26 TNA: E 372/124 rots. 19–30d; E 372/145 rots. 22–40d.
27 TNA: E 372/134 rot. 1d [image 1118]; E 372/139 rot. 21 [image 2241].
28 TNA: E 372/98 rot. 6d [image 8291]; E 372/105 rot. 17d [image 8838].
29 Public Record Office, *List of Foreign Accounts Enrolled on the Great Rolls of the Exchequer*, Lists and Indexes No. 11, (London: HMSO, 1900).
30 Wild, ed., *Wardrobe Accounts*.
31 See for instance Martin Allen, *Mints and Money in Medieval England* (Cambridge: Cambridge University Press, 2012). In appendixes C and D he uses the pipe roll accounts to construct detailed tables of mint output and profit from 1220 to 1544.
32 Margaret Howell, *Regalian Right in Medieval England* (London: Athlone Press, 1962), 229.
33 For instance, just in 1258, the priors and convents of Whitby, St Mary's York, and Westminster all fined to retain custody during vacancies: *CFR 1257–58*, nos. 294 and 600; 1258–59, no. 81.
34 Scott L. Waugh, "The Origins of the Office of Escheator," In *The Growth of Royal Government under Henry III*, edited by David Crook and Louise J. Wilkinson (Woodbridge: Boydell Press, 2015).
35 TNA series E 136, Escheators' Particulars of Account.
36 TNA: E 372/124 rot. 30d [image 8181].
37 The later accounts are in TNA series E 356. There is a detailed calendar of the accounts for this period: Stuart Jenks, ed., *The Enrolled Customs Accounts Part 1*, List & Index Society 303 (Kew, 2004). As the customs accounts in the pipe rolls are not covered by the PRO *List of Foreign Accounts*, it may be worth mentioning here that they can be found in these rolls: TNA: E 372/124, 125, 133, 134, 143, 145, 146, and 149.
38 Mabel H. Mills, "Exchequer Agenda and Estimate of Revenue, Easter Term 1284," *EHR* 40, 158 (1925): 229–34.
39 Mabel H. Mills, "Review of James H. Ramsay, A History of the Revenues of the Kings of England, 1066–1399," *EHR* 41, 163 (1926): 429.
40 Dorothea Oschinsky, *Walter of Henley and Other Treatises on Estate Management and Accounting* (Oxford: Clarendon Press, 1971), 214. Noël Denholm-Young, *Seignorial Administration in England*, Oxford Historical Series, (London: Oxford University Press, 1937), 50, 126–7. On official accountability, see John Sabapathy, *Officers and Accountability in Medieval England, 1170–1300* (Oxford: Oxford University Press, 2014), chapters 2 (bailiffs and stewards), 3 (sheriffs).
41 Stacey, *Politics, Policy, and Finance*, 226.

4 An example
The 1259 pipe roll

Pipe rolls can be off-putting, due to their unwieldy size, the use of highly abbreviated Latin, and an absence of clear signposts to indicate where you are in the text. The best way to learn how to find your way around a pipe roll is to take a sample roll, and to see how it is put together. They are all physically similar, and their contents also follow similar patterns, best explained with examples from a fairly typical roll. At the risk of some repetition, this should show how the components of the pipe roll, described in the previous chapters, were used in practice. An actual roll can also help to make the abbreviated Latin less mysterious: a photo of the original roll can be compared with a transcription which expands the abbreviations, as a sort of Rosetta Stone which will make it easier to understand other rolls.

The example, and where to find it

We can use the 1259 pipe roll, TNA: E 372/103, as a suitable example. It is the roll for a significant year, the first full year of government by the baronial council which seized power in the spring of 1258.[1] It is convenient for our purposes, because both a transcription and a set of photographs are freely available online. The transcription can be found as the appendix to a King's College London PhD thesis, which can be downloaded from either the British Library or King's College London. The photographs of the roll are on the Anglo-American Legal Tradition (AALT) website.[2] The transcription will also be available in print, in a Pipe Roll Society volume, with introduction and indexes, to be published in 2024. Both online and in print, the transcription is presented as numbered paragraphs, and these numbers are used for the references in parentheses below.

To begin at the beginning, at the top of the first rotulet is the year, *Anno xliij R.H.*, so we already have something to interpret. It is the roll for year 43 of the reign of king Henry III, in other words 1258–59. For the Exchequer, that meant the year ending at Michaelmas, 29 September 1259.

This roll is made up of twenty-three rotulets, and it records the accounts for twenty-four counties, or pairs of counties. Nine of these accounts cover two years, 1257–59, and several counties are omitted, probably because of a lack of time to complete the audit process. The omissions include Wiltshire, Lancashire, and Bedfordshire and Buckinghamshire, which all accounted in the following year's roll. In this year's roll, there are no foreign accounts – that is, accounts for institutions other than the counties. There are some 213,500 words of Latin text, in about 5,300 entries, many of which cover more than one individual debt or payment. Most entries simply list outstanding debts, but the roll records some 1,800 transactions in which cash was paid. These transactions produced around £21,600; details of the sources and destinations of this revenue are given below.

The county accounts all follow much the same pattern, which is best described by going through the components of a single county's account. We can then look at some of the less obvious features of the text.

A county account: Northamptonshire

The Northamptonshire account is on rotulet 5 of the roll, beginning at entry 977 of the transcript, and from image 1675 on the AALT website. The account begins with the name of the county, *Norhamptun'*, which is close enough to Northampton(shire) to leave little doubt as to its identity. Place-names have of course changed since 1259, and they are spelled in numerous ways in the pipe roll (consistency was evidently not a major consideration for the Exchequer clerks). Nevertheless, they are often close enough to modern forms for guess-work to be checked in one of the dictionaries of place-names, or, in much more detail, in the county volumes of the English Place-Name Society.[3]

Each county's account begins in much the same way: the sheriff accounts for the county farm, and for the amount which he has paid into the Treasury. In this case (977), Eustace of Watford, as custodian, accounts for (*reddit compotum de*, almost always abbreviated to *r.c. de*) some £230. He has paid nothing into the Treasury. The farm was a fixed amount, which had been unchanged since the late twelfth century. The system had become fossilized, failing to respond to inflation and to the removal of the royal demesne properties from the sheriffs' control.

The outdated nature of the farm becomes plain in the next paragraph (978), listing all the properties which no longer contributed to the farm, known as *terre date*, literally the lands which had been given. Some of these towns and manors had been farmed out (leased for a fixed annual payment), and would now account separately. An example of those listed is Brigstock; the roll says that it had contributed £10 a year to the farm, and that the men of the vill would answer for it below. Some lands had simply been granted as gifts or on easy terms, to favoured individuals or religious institutions. In either case, they no longer formed part of the farm. The net amount, the fixed farm minus these deductions *in terris datis*, was known as the 'body of the county', *corpus comitatus*, the initial sum which the sheriff had to produce. For Northamptonshire, the farm of £230 was reduced to a *corpus* of just £4 13s. 10d.

48 *An example*

After the farm and the *terre date*, the county account then moves on to the sheriff's expenditure, which has to be set against his income (979). Some expenses are fixed, recurring every year, listed as *elemosina constituta*. Every county, for example, makes a small annual payment to the Templars; some pay annual fees for chaplains, or royal servants. There are also the payments specific to that year, which can cover almost any activity which the sheriff might be ordered to perform. Because these expenses are variable, they are one of the more interesting features of pipe rolls, sometimes covering very unlikely items: in the 1257 pipe roll, the sheriffs of London claimed the costs of maintaining the king's elephant in the Tower of London.[4] The sheriff of Northamptonshire in 1259 recorded more mundane expenses: repairing the wall around the king's park outside Northampton; the upkeep of the king's falcons and greyhounds at Geddington; the repair of the gaol in Northampton castle; and the maintenance of approvers, convicted criminals who informed on their accomplices. At the end of the list of expenses, the roll gives the total £30 6s. 2½d. of expenditure, which is to be set against the sheriff's sources of revenue: £4 13s. 10d. from the remainder of the farm, and the rest from the profit of the county.

As a custodian, Eustace was obliged to report all the revenue he had collected. The next paragraph (980) deals with the profit, the revenue over and above the farm which the sheriff was traditionally expected to produce. This was an attempt to extract a more realistic amount from the sheriffs than the antiquated farm. Eustace reported a profit of £86. He had paid £30 to the Treasury, spent £26 on the expenses in the previous paragraph, and owed £30.

After the current sheriff's farm, expenses, and profit, there are entries for arrears owed by previous sheriffs (981–84), then a series of payments for various properties which have been farmed out (985–1000). Some of these are among the *terre date* which once contributed to the county farm. The bulk of the county entries which take up the rest of this rotulet are outstanding debts which have been copied from the previous year's roll. The process was much the same in every county. Unpaid debts were copied from one roll to the next. Payments towards these debts were recorded, and once they had been paid in full, they no longer needed to be copied, and dropped out. New debts were added at the end. This meant that, roughly speaking, the oldest debts were towards the top and the newest at the bottom of the county's account. In the case of Northamptonshire, there are some very old outstanding debts, one said to derive from roll 14 of king John – that is, 1213 (1005). Eustace of Watford himself owed £1,238 from debts contained in the 1221 roll (1002). Debts for fines and amercements imposed many years ago are jumbled together with recurring payments, such as the farm of Brigstock (1064), which was among the *terre date*.

The list of old debts goes on for the whole of the face of the rotulet, broken by headings, also copied from roll to roll over many years. Such headings refer to amercements imposed for forest offences (1057) or by justices in eyre

An example

(1075) and are followed by any outstanding debts for these amercements, before the list of miscellaneous outstanding debts continues. That apart, there is nothing to help one navigate through the long sequence of debts, and a few payments. At the foot of the face of this rotulet, there is a note indicating that the account continues on the reverse, and a feint rotulet number in pencil. This numbering, presumably relatively modern, often barely visible, is found in many rolls. The list of old debts continues onto the dorse of the rotulet. In the lower half of the dorse there is the heading *De oblatis* (1181). This heading is found in every county account, and it introduces the series of debts copied from the immediately preceding roll. It is followed by another heading, *Nova oblata* (1204), which introduces the new debts which are appearing in the roll for the first time.

The county account is too long for a single rotulet, and at the foot of the dorse there is a note to indicate that the remainder can be found after the account for Devon. This was the usual way of dealing with continuations, to fit them into spare space left over after another county's accounts. There is also an endorsement, in a large bold hand, of the county name, upside-down. These endorsements at the foot of each dorse serve as a navigation aid, to find the appropriate rotulet when the roll is rolled up.

Details of the county account

Blanching

Many sums of money in the roll are written with the note *bl.* after them – for example, the county farm (977) and many of the *terre date* (978). This indicates that they have been blanched. Blanching was a convention, indicating that the stated sum needed to be increased by a shilling in the pound, or one-twentieth. This is sometimes spelled out, as in the calculation of the *corpus comitatus* at the end of entry 978: the sheriff owes £4 9s. 4d. bl., which is increased to £4 13s. 10d. (which does indeed work out as 1,072d. plus a twentieth, 54d., making 1,126d.) Occasionally, sums of money are followed by *num.*, meaning by number: this is usually found in calculations involving the conversion of blanched amounts to actual sums, which could be expressed as a number of coins (990).

Marginal notes

Throughout the roll, there are brief marginal notes against many entries, usually to the left of the first word. These notes appear to have been added to the roll, either during the auditing process or when a later year's roll was being drawn up. The most common note is *f*: this is found repeatedly, and 'probably stands for *fecit* and implies that the sheriff has levied the debt and is therefore answerable for it.'[5] Another common annotation is *t*, found either in the margin or above the name of a debtor, for instance in entry 1213. This was added to the roll in the following year, if the debt had been collected in full (*totum*); the clerk could thus avoid having to write out the details again. Instead, the next year's roll simply reported that the sheriff accounted for so much money from the debts of several people whose names were marked with the letter *t* in the preceding roll (1153).

Custodian and farmer sheriffs

At the beginning of this county account, Eustace of Watford is said to account as a custodian (*ut custos*). This meant that he simply collected and reported the revenues of the county, delivering the cash to the Treasury and receiving a fixed payment for his services (in his case 40 marks, which he did not receive until 1266).[6] Most of the sheriffs of 1258–59 were appointed as custodians, but this was unusual. The normal practice was for a farmer sheriff to agree to pay a fixed sum, originally the county farm, and later a fixed profit as well: if he collected more than the agreed sum, he kept it; if less, that was his problem – he still had to pay the agreed farm and profit. Custodians were appointed from time to time, perhaps as a check on the amount of revenue which a county might realistically be expected to produce. In the circumstances of 1258–59, the appointment of custodians could also be a response to discontent about the excessive levels of profit required from farmer sheriffs, who were accused of squeezing the counties.

Payment by instalments

Several entries in the roll include a note near the right margin: *Per annum* and a sum of money. These are debts which have been 'attermed' – the Exchequer has agreed that the debt should be paid off by annual instalments. For instance, the nuns of Delapré abbey (1039) owed £7 4s. 5d. They had paid 20s. and now owed £6 4s. 5d. This entry has a note to the right, *Per annum* 20s. Such arrangements could be very generous. Eustace of Watford himself owed £1,238, which he was paying off at 5 marks (£3 6s. 8d.) a year (1002). At that rate, it would have taken 372 years to complete payment!

The roll and revenue

The total revenue recorded in this pipe roll, from all the counties covered, can be assigned, very roughly, to the categories shown in Table 4.1. This demonstrates that the traditional revenues making up the county farm and profit were no longer the most significant source of royal income. The boroughs and manors, many of which had once formed part of the county farm, contributed much more. Northamptonshire provides the examples of the boroughs of Northampton, farmed by the burgesses for £120 a year (985), and Corby, with a farm of £8 *bl*. plus an increment of 40s. (990–1). The manors include Brigstock: this was once part of the farm, and is listed in the *terre date*

Table 4.1 Sources of revenue, 1259 pipe roll

	£	£
County revenues:		
net county farm	1,210	
profit and increment	710	
farm, etc. from previous years	860	
Total		2,780
Amercements		1,910
Boroughs		4,130
Debts		2,680
Forests		310
Manors, etc.		3,370
Offerings & fines		3,540
Taxes		500
Other		2,410
Total		**21,630**

Table 4.2 Application of revenue, 1259 pipe roll

	£
Treasury	12,850
Wardrobe	580
Building works	2,090
Charity & religion	790
Food & drink	500
Hunting, animals	20
Individuals	2,750
Justice	80
Military	110
Supplies & transport	480
Other	1,380
Total	**21,630**

with a value of £10 *bl.*; the roll shows that it was now farmed by the men of Brigstock for £40. The same had happened to the manors of Geddington, Kingsthorpe, and Silverstone, all farmed by their inhabitants (1064–7). The other major sources were payments described simply as debts (the origins of such debts could only be identified by tracking them back through preceding pipe rolls), and fines and amercements, described in more detail below.

As we have seen with the Northamptonshire county revenues, some of the cash which was collected was sent to the Treasury, and some spent locally, as instructed by central government. Some cash was also delivered directly to the Wardrobe, which controlled the finances of the royal household. The destination of revenues included in the 1259 roll is shown in Table 4.2. More than half the total went to the Treasury, and the major categories of local expenditure were payments to individuals and building works. The individuals receiving such cash ranged from royal servants to officials such as judges, and royal friends and relations whom the king wished to favour.

County farm and profit

The county farm and profit appear at first sight to be the most important parts of each county's account: they are the first items to appear after the heading giving the name of the county. In them, the sheriff accounts for the sums due and the amounts paid into the Treasury and spent locally. In fact, as Table 4.1 shows, by 1259 the current year's farm and profit made up only about a tenth of total pipe roll revenue. We have already seen one reason for the reduced significance of the farm: the removal of the royal demesne boroughs and manors from the sheriff's custody. The deduction of the sums attributed to the *terre date*, which were merely nominal values dating back to the twelfth century, left a remainder, the net figure for the farm, known as the *corpus comitatus*.

There had been attempts to compensate for the growing irrelevance of the farm, and the erosion of its real value by inflation. Sheriffs were required to produce fixed sums for profit (and in a few counties, also an increment), and the level of profit was increased over time. But the pipe rolls, while recording the amounts set for farm and profit, did not show how these amounts were made up. They only showed the sums which were *not* included – the *terre date* deducted from the farm. We can only see details of the sheriffs' sources of revenue when the sheriffs were appointed as custodians and had to account in detail for the money they had collected. Most of the sheriffs of 1258–59 were custodians and had to produce particulars of account, eighteen of which survive. Unfortunately, only a few extracts from these accounts have been published, but the manuscript records indicate where the sheriffs' income came from.

In the case of Northamptonshire, the record is very straightforward.[7] The sheriff, Eustace of Watford, reported income under only two headings: the fixed fines collected from the hundreds, the administrative sub-divisions of the county, amounting to £60 11s. 8d.; and the income from pleas at the county court, a total of £30 3s. 10d. The latter amount derived from a long list of individuals, most of whom had paid relatively small sums, as low as 6d., for such offences as brewing against the assize, unjust detention, trespass, or simply default. There were also many amercements for procedural offences, such as failure to prosecute and failure to attend the court. The account ends with the calculation of the total, apparently added in another hand, perhaps at the Exchequer after the sheriff had submitted his particulars: the total was £90 15s., from which £4 13s. 10d. should be deducted to make up the *corpus* of the county; the remainder was £86 14d., for which the sheriff answered in the pipe roll. These figures are indeed repeated in the pipe roll, which gives the same amounts for the *corpus* and the profit of the county, respectively.

An example 53

Each county is different. The accounts were produced locally, so there is no common approach to layout or the amount of detail reported. While Northamptonshire just gave a long list of names and amercements, other counties itemized the date and place of each county and hundred court, with sub-totals for the relevant fines and amercements. The sources of income also varied widely. They all have lists of amercements, mostly fairly trivial and repetitive (although there are exceptions, about which one would like to know more: in Kent John Ealdegrom was amerced 6*d.* because he beat his mother). In several counties, the profits of justice are joined by a variety of traditional impositions, generally collected at the county and hundred courts, under such names as hidage, view of frankpledge, wardpenny, and sheriff's aid. A few counties had idiosyncratic sources of income: a fixed rent of hens in Berkshire; cod, haddock, and herrings in Northumberland; stray sows in Nottinghamshire; and a customary harvest due in Somerset.[8]

This detail is irrelevant to the pipe roll. It is only concerned with the overall amount of cash produced, and how it compares with the sum expected for the *corpus*. In most years, when there were farmer sheriffs, the detail behind the farm and profit was invisible, because the sheriffs did not need to explain the sources of the cash they collected.

Fines in 1259

Fines make up a major part of the debts in the pipe roll, and the fine rolls, available online, provide additional information about these entries.[9] Fines were offers of payment to the king, in cash or in commodities such as hawks, horses, or wine. In return, the king was expected to provide a specified benefit: this could be a favour, like the right to hold a market, or a more routine concession, like the issue of a judicial writ. The Chancery, the writing office which travelled with the king, recorded the fines on the fine rolls. They were then copied onto the originalia rolls which were sent to the Exchequer. The Exchequer could sort the fines by county, include lists of the amounts to be collected in the summons sent to the appropriate sheriff, and record the new debts in the *Nova oblata* section of the pipe roll.

The Northamptonshire *Nova oblata* in the 1259 pipe roll illustrate this process. There are twelve fines from the 1257–58 fine roll, and twenty fines from the 1258–59 fine roll, grouped together in entries 1206–13 of the pipe roll. A couple of examples may show how information about fines was transferred. On 15 July 1258, Thomas de Beseville offered half a mark for taking an assize of novel disseisin (an action for the recovery of property) before the justice Gilbert of Preston. The fine roll records that the appropriate order for holding the assize was sent to the sheriff of Northamptonshire, and that the fine was copied onto the originalia roll, to be sent to the Exchequer. The Exchequer then recorded a brief version in the pipe roll, stating only that Beseville owed half a mark for having an assize (1211).[10] Similarly, on 30 March 1259, Adam Fleming offered one mark for a writ *ad terminum*

54 *An example*

(a writ which provided for a plea to be heard before a certain court at a certain time); again the order was sent to the sheriff, and the offer recorded in the originalia. In this case, the entry in the originalia must have been transferred fairly rapidly to the summons sent to the sheriff, because the pipe roll shows that he accounted for this sum, for having an unspecified writ, and had paid it into the Treasury together with various other debts, in a lump sum payment of £13 10s. (1210). The fine and originalia rolls could also record arrangements to pay debts by instalments, as was done by the former sheriff William de Lisle, who was to pay the £250 debt in entry 1533 at 40 marks a year.[11]

Profits of justice

As Table 4.1 shows, the amercements, or financial penalties, imposed by the royal courts were a major contributor to pipe roll income. Debts for amercements were originally listed in detail in the pipe rolls, but the number of such debts became far too great to be copied in full into the rolls. Instead, the Exchequer relied on the estreat rolls. These were the rolls listing outstanding fines and amercements imposed by the courts, which the justices sent to the Exchequer at the end of judicial proceedings. They also showed the sums which should be paid to the holders of certain liberties, who had the right to receive amercements imposed on their tenants. The Exchequer usually just noted in the pipe rolls that the debts and liberties from a particular court's proceedings had not been copied into the roll. Such notes occur frequently in every county's account, usually in a smaller hand than the bulk of the entries, towards the right margin.

In Northamptonshire in the 1259 roll, there are several notes about debts and liberties from various courts. The most important was the eyre, the visitation of the justices who travelled from county to county to hear outstanding civil and criminal cases, in principle visiting each county every seven years or so. Northamptonshire had been visited in 1247 by justices led by Roger Thirkleby (1075, 1080), and in 1253 by Simon Walton (1115, 1124). There was then the special eyre of the justiciar Hugh Bigod, who came to Northamptonshire in July-September 1258 (1205).[12] Only particularly large or significant amercements were copied from the estreat into the pipe roll, and for the bulk of the debts, the pipe roll simply recorded the overall amount collected by the sheriff. In the case of Bigod's eyre, still recent, the pipe roll showed that the sheriff accounted for £6 16s. 8d. for the amercements of various people whose names were marked with the letter *t* in a roll of amercements before Hugh Bigod, and £4 1m. for amercements in another such roll (1210). There is no further detail in the pipe roll to tell us how many amercements, from whom, these lump sums covered. In the account of another county, Lincolnshire, there are entries both for a lump sum to be collected from those marked with a *t* in the roll of amercements (1502) and for an individual amercement. John de Neville owed £100 for trespass, as shown in the roll of amercements before Hugh Bigod, marked Lincolnshire (1507).

In the records of Bigod's eyre, we can find this case: it was found that John de Neville had raised an embankment, blocking the path to Richard of Healing's mill; the path was to be opened and the embankment knocked down at John's expense, and he was 'in mercy' – liable to the financial penalty which was set subsequently.[13] The pipe roll gives us only part of the story, and the full circumstances have to be sought in the court records, if they survive.

The marking-up with *t* for *totum* took place in the estreat roll. At the same time, outstanding debts were marked *d* in the estreat. In following years, the outstanding debts would be chased up, and when they were paid a *t* would be added to the estreat roll entry, which would thus be marked *td*. There was an elaborate procedure of marking up the estreat rolls with dots to show the number of times a particular debt had been summoned, which was also recorded in the pipe roll when older debts were collected. For example, the sheriff accounted in 1259 for £10 16s. 8d. of debts from Walton's eyre of 1253, as amercements of people whose names were marked with a letter *t* and a letter *d* with three dots over them in the roll of that eyre (1123). The three dots are also included above the *t* in the pipe roll entry.[14]

The same approach was followed for amercements from other types of court, such as the forest eyre (1057–60, 1197–203), the bench (1428), and the king's council (1432). A few debts for amercements were set out in full in the pipe roll, while the sheriff accounted for a lump sum for the remaining unspecified amercements which had been marked up in the roll produced by the court. The profits of justice could also include the proceeds of the chattels of fugitives and those who had been hanged, as in the entry for gaol delivery at Lincoln (1524), similarly included in the lump sum produced by the sheriff. The pipe roll simply recorded that debts for amercements were not in the roll (1434).

Pipe roll timetable

The pipe roll itself does not show how it was produced. For the stages in its production, and the annual schedule, we have to look at another set of Exchequer records, the memoranda rolls. Two memoranda rolls were produced each year, for the King's Remembrancer and Lord Treasurer, and at this period they were largely identical. Few memoranda rolls have been edited and published, but fortunately, photographs of both sets of rolls are on the AALT website.[15]

The pipe roll nominally covers the year which began on the day after Michaelmas, 30 September 1258, the day when the mayor and citizens of London presented their sheriffs for the year at the Exchequer. There was some delay before the rest of the sheriffs were appointed. This may well have been caused by the governing council's discussions about plans for local government reform, which led to the production of the Ordinance of Sheriffs on 20 October. This proclamation, sent to every county, set out requirements for sheriffs to be fair and uncorrupt, not taking bribes or exploiting the counties.

At about the same time, the Chancery used the originalia roll to inform the Exchequer of the appointment of twenty new sheriffs.[16]

In November, the new sheriffs were summoned to the Exchequer to take the oath of office and began work. In some cases the memoranda roll records that their predecessors were ordered to hand over summonses, rolls, and writs, so that the new sheriffs would know about the debts which they were expected to collect. The summonses were supposed to be sent to each sheriff twice a year, listing the debts that had been extracted from the originalia rolls, estreats, and past pipe rolls as needing collection within their county. They must have been lengthy documents – in December 1258 the sheriff of Lincolnshire was sent a large summons containing eight membranes, as well as a small summons from the originalia of 1257–58. The sheriffs evidently set to work quite quickly, making the first deliveries of cash payments to the Treasury early in 1259. On 18 January, the new sheriff of Hampshire delivered nearly £3,000 from the revenues of the vacant bishopric of Winchester. In February, the sheriffs of Oxfordshire, Wiltshire, and Yorkshire made 'dividend' payments. These were lump sums covering numerous debts from their counties, for which the sheriff received a single tally stick as a receipt.[17]

The first formal event of the sheriffs' year was the *adventus*, after Easter, when sheriffs and some boroughs were expected to come to the Exchequer with the revenues of the preceding half-year. The proceeds were noted in the memoranda roll. In fact, most of the sheriffs were represented by their clerks, and in some cases, they brought nothing but writs, but even so this *adventus*, on 21 April 1259, produced £1,644. In the course of the Easter term, several sheriffs were summoned for the view of their accounts, a sort of interim report. There was no detailed record of the view, but it presumably gave the Exchequer an indication of how the sheriffs were performing, and of the cash they were likely to produce. It also gave the Exchequer an opportunity to issue instructions as to the debts to be pursued.[18]

The year ended at Michaelmas, and the next day, the morrow of Michaelmas or 30 September 1259, there was the Michaelmas *adventus*. The sheriffs and boroughs brought £2,062, from the revenues of the second half of the year. Of course, cash sums were delivered before and after each *adventus*. The Exchequer's receipt rolls show that the amounts shown in the record of the *adventus* were actually received into the Treasury over several following weeks. The *adventus* might thus be regarded as a report of the sums that sheriffs and boroughs had declared that they would pay. Some performed more promptly than others. On this occasion, for example, the sheriff of Devon is said to have brought £11 profit; the receipt roll records that he paid in this sum on 1 October. The sheriff of Herefordshire was represented by his clerk, who brought £20 profit; but this payment was not recorded in the receipt roll until 18 October.[19]

The process of auditing the county accounts and compiling the pipe roll also began immediately after Michaelmas, on 30 September. The timetable, known as the *dies dati*, was set out in the memoranda roll, allowing a week or more for each county, marked up as the audits progressed: Cumberland, 30 September, accounted; Cambridgeshire, 6 October, accounted; Northumberland, 13 October, postponed to 12 April; and so on. The list ended with Northamptonshire on 22 July, accounted, then Wiltshire on 29 July, but did not account before Michaelmas, and Bedfordshire, for which no date was set because there was not enough time. There was even an attempt to catch up with the accounts of Cornwall, which had not reported since 1241–42 (because the county had been granted to the king's brother, Earl Richard of Cornwall).[20] The list of *dies dati* shows that the audit process occupied most of the year, complicated by appointments being deferred, sometimes more than once. It was not completed. The counties left over, like Wiltshire and Bedfordshire, were audited in 1260–61 for two years' accounts. It may be worth noting that the order in which the counties appear in the pipe roll is not the order in which they were audited: the first to be audited, Cumberland, is on rotulet 15, followed by Cambridgeshire; Hampshire, on rotulet 1, was audited on 14 January; and the last to be audited, Northamptonshire, is on rotulets 5, 6, and 7. The rotulets must have been kept loose, with unused areas filled in by continuations of later counties, and only sewn together when the audits were completed. This led to the necessity to jump around in the completed roll, to find the separated sections of a single county's account; these are introduced by words such as *Residuum* or *Item*, or *Adhuc residuum* for a second continuation.

As the audit process ran for most of the year following the year which the pipe roll nominally covered, the accounts of the later counties to be audited could include transactions from some time after the supposed year end. Northamptonshire, last to be audited, thus included in the 1259 pipe roll payments for having a writ by Joanna le Estreys (1176) and Adam Fleming (1210); the receipt roll records these payments on 28 February 1260, five months after the end of the 1258–59 Exchequer year.[21]

Pipe rolls and receipt rolls

The Exchequer's receipt rolls recorded the payments of cash received by the Treasury. At least in principle, one set of rolls, drawn up as a single column of payments, recorded cash receipts in chronological order, with sub-totals for each day and each week of the Exchequer term. It is possible that these rolls sometimes deferred recording payments which arrived in instalments, only noting them when they were completed by the final instalment. Nevertheless, they give at least an indication of the way cash flowed in to the Treasury, day by day. Another set of rolls, laid out in three columns, recorded the details of lump sum payments, county by county rather than chronologically. It is sometimes possible to relate payments recorded in the pipe rolls to the payments found in the receipt rolls. On the other hand, many payments simply cannot be matched up: there are the problems of timing, when payments were made before or after the year nominally covered by the pipe roll; and the fact that the chronological receipt rolls record lump sum payments by sheriffs and others as totals, without giving any indication of the individual transactions which these sums cover.

Northamptonshire can again provide examples, this time for the difficulty of tracking payments. The three-column receipt roll for the Easter term of 1259 has two entries under the Northamptonshire heading. One is for 4*m*. 5*s*. received from the abbot of Evesham for a farm; this can be found in the pipe roll (1111) as payment for the farm of Fawsley hundred. The other is more complex, a group of sixteen payments from named individuals, delivered by John Sampson, bailiff of Northampton. Most of these payments, mostly just 12*d*. or 2*s*. for false measure, and some larger amounts for wine or cloth sold against the assize, seem to be market offences. They add up to £5 2*s*. 4*d*. In the chronological receipt roll for that term, there is a payment on 22 April 1259 of £5 40*d*. from the men of Northampton *per dividenda* – that is, a lump sum payment on behalf of several individuals.[22] There is a shilling difference between these two sums, but they are close enough to make it likely that they refer to the same transaction, with a minor mathematical or copying error. The problem is to find them in the pipe roll. Just one payment from the receipt roll list is recorded individually in the pipe roll: Hugh de la Quarrer', 40*d*. for having a writ (1091). The rest are not to be found, so they must have been subsumed in the lump sum payments by the sheriff for market amercements (1228, 1230).

Northamptonshire entries in the chronological receipt rolls also make imperfect matches with the pipe roll. John Lovel is shown in the pipe roll to have paid 100*s*. for 'trespass of venison' – a forest offence (1436). He is in the receipt rolls three times, each time paying 2½*m*. for forest trespass, on 28 April and 15 October 1259, and 23 June 1260. This adds up to 100*s*., with the last payment having been made a few weeks before the Northamptonshire account was audited, so that the total could appear as a single transaction in the 1258–59 pipe roll.[23] The sheriff, Eustace of Watford, paid £30 on 22 April 1259 for the profit of the county, which fits nicely with the pipe roll entry for profit (980). It is not so simple to allocate his dividend payments of £10 on 26 May, and £33 ½*m*. on 30 September.[24] These must represent some of the numerous entries in the pipe roll where the sheriff is paying in lump sums for fines and amercements; they are not itemized in the three-column receipt roll, so in this case there is no way of relating one set of rolls to the other.

Despite these problems, the chronological receipt rolls provide a clear insight into the annual rhythm of payments arriving in the Treasury. The significance of the *adventus* is clear in the rolls showing the amounts received by the Exchequer from the morrow of Michaelmas 1258 to Michaelmas 1259. Over the whole year, the Exchequer received almost £15,000 in cash. Nearly £3,000 came from a single source, early in January: revenues from the bishopric of Winchester, which the governing council treated as if it was vacant, following the flight of the bishop-elect. This was a unique bonus for the hard-pressed government, but the rest of the year followed the usual pattern. The first four weeks after Michaelmas, including the *adventus*, produced some £3,450. Receipts then tailed off for the rest of the term and did not pick up again until the new term started after Easter. Again, the *adventus* and the following four weeks produced a major influx of cash, some £3,500. So a large proportion of the government's routine cash income was produced around the time of these two events.

Pipe roll and memoranda roll accounts

As each county was audited, a list of outstanding debts in the memoranda roll was marked up. These lists in the memoranda roll can be compared to the evidence of the pipe roll, to show what happened when the sheriff came to account. If we return to Northamptonshire as an example, it was audited last, and its account is the last in the memoranda roll.[25] It is a single membrane, headed 'Account of Northamptonshire for 1258–59, presented at the Exchequer on 22 July 1260 by Eustace of Watford, sheriff'. This is followed by a long list, beginning with 'The same sheriff' and his two predecessors, then some 90 short entries, each giving a name, a debt and the reason for the debt. These entries are in the same order as they appear in the pipe roll, starting with 'Robert Basset, £10 19s. 3½d. for three debts' (983) and ending with 'Robert de Mares, 16m. for the farm of Porchester castle' (1199). The last entries in the memoranda roll list are to be found in the *De oblatis* section of the pipe roll, the debts which were added to the pipe roll in the previous year. This implies that the memoranda roll list was drawn up by going through the previous pipe roll and selecting the debts which were to be pursued.

Many of the names in the memoranda roll have been annotated, usually very briefly. The most common note is simply '*dis.*' – distrain, meaning to seize the debtor's chattels, usually livestock, to enforce payment. There are also variants such as 'distrain the tenants of his lands' and 'distrain so that the sheriff delivers the money to the king's Wardrobe on 22 August'. Comparison with the pipe roll shows that these are debts which had not yet been paid. A few outstanding debts had been paid, such as those of Walter parson of Wootton (1071) and Peter of Irchester (1073) for forest offences; these are marked 'paid all' in the memoranda roll. Some were partially paid, like the debt of the burgesses of Northampton for £16 8s. 6d. (1148); the memoranda roll notes 'they have paid 10 marks, distrain for the remainder'.

There are many other notes, transferring debts to another county, ordering the sheriff to enter the town of Northampton to distrain for debts, or recording whether the terms for attermed debts were being observed. From these notes, we can imagine the memoranda roll list serving as the agenda for the audit. The bulk of the pipe roll account for the county had been written in advance, leaving blank spaces to be filled in between the names of debtors and the amounts owed. The list starts with the sheriff himself, then the arrears of his predecessors, just as the entries appear at the beginning of the pipe roll county account, so presumably these were dealt with first. The audit would then go through the long list of outstanding debts. For each debt, there was a note added to the memoranda roll as to whether it had yet been paid, and if not, what the sheriff was to do about it. Similarly, the corresponding pipe roll entries were filled in with the details of payments made: the gap between name and amount would be filled with the phrase 'accounts for' (*r.c. de*); towards the right margin, there was added the note 'Delivered to the Treasury. He or she is quit'. Where no payment had been received, the gap was left empty.

Sheriffs were not the only officials involved in the audit: there is a note that the sheriff is to take the town of Northampton into the king's hand, because they had not sent their bailiff to the sheriff's account. At the end of the list in the memoranda roll, there is a note of the amount which the sheriff still owed, known as the sum. The sheriff had to pledge payment to the marshal of the Exchequer, and he was given a day to pay or to set out the expenses he should be allowed. For Eustace of Watford, the day for settling his debt was given as 30 September 1260, so it was a full year after the end of the period to which it related. Other debts went on much longer: the sheriff of Kent paid £10 for the remainder of the county farm from 1258–59 on 9 July 1261. In most cases, late payments were allowed, and sometimes repeatedly deferred, under the oath to the marshal. Occasionally, the Exchequer took a harsher approach: the sheriff of Cumberland, the first to be audited on 30 September 1259, owed a sum of £203; he gave his pledge to the marshal for that money and was given a day to pay on 13 October as a prisoner (*ut priso*).[26]

The pipe roll and current events

The year 1258–59 was unusually eventful, but this would not be immediately apparent from the pipe roll. It completely ignored one major event, the great famine of 1258, one of the worst in English history. This was a disaster, caused by bad weather and successive crop failures, which led to food shortages and a major rise in prices. The chronicler Matthew Paris reported:

> With grain being scarce, an innumerable multitude of poor people died. And their bodies were found everywhere, swollen by hunger. . . . And when many dead bodies were found, large and wide ditches were made in the cemeteries, in which very many people's bodies were laid.[27]

There is no mention of the famine in the pipe roll. There is also no explicit reference to the fact that a council had taken control of government, ending Henry III's personal rule, and embarked on a programme of reform. The fact that most of the sheriffs accounted as custodians was unusual, but not unprecedented. The council's expectations for their honesty and fairness were not apparent in the pipe roll, which was only concerned with their financial performance. Current events are only glimpsed incidentally, among the expenses which were set against county revenues.

Some sheriffs and boroughs were still claiming for expenditure on preparations for the king's planned campaign in north Wales in 1258. This had been abandoned, but not before some costs had been incurred: the carriage of the king's pavilions from Tamworth to Chester (2848); buying and carrying 300 salted salmon from Carlisle to Chester for the army (3059); 100 quarters of oats bought at Worcester and transported to Newcastle under Lyme (3332); galleys to be built at Dunwich and Yarmouth (5128–9).

There were also expenses reflecting diplomatic activity. The bishop of Worcester received 50 marks for his expenses on a mission to Germany, with a further 10 marks for his passage and return through Kent (3352, 2048); this may be a reference to his journey to France and Germany in 1257, to see Richard of Cornwall, the king's brother, who had been elected king of the Romans. The bishop was sent to discuss a proposed treaty with France. Another ecclesiastic received expenses for a mission to Richard, this time the abbot of St Edmunds who met him at St Omer in January 1259 (5090). The treaty with France, the Treaty of Paris, was finalized at the end of 1259. Henry III went to France in November 1259, shortly after the end of the year nominally covered by the pipe roll.[28] The sheriff of Kent had to pay £9 for the repair of bridges in readiness for the king's crossing (2195).

There are a few other examples of expenditure related to events of the year, but they add little to what we might learn from Chancery records and chronicles. The sheriff of Hampshire had to pay for the carriage to Westminster of the revenues of the bishopric of Winchester (3); the bishop-elect, the king's half-brother, had fled the country, allowing the governing council to take control of his very rich see. The sheriffs of London found an escort of serjeants to convey Walter de Scotney to Winchester, where he was executed for attempting to poison the earl of Gloucester (2250). Simon and Eleanor de Montfort were to receive manors in several counties worth 600 marks a year, to replace the cash payments which they had previously received for Eleanor's dower; this seems to be the only instance in the roll of a glancing reference to the new regime, stating that the king made this decision by the counsel of his magnates (4481). These incidental glimpses are all that the pipe roll affords. It is concerned with debts and payments, so it only touches on the events of politics and diplomacy when they happen to require expenditure to be set against the revenues recorded in the roll.

The pipe roll and local and family history

There is plenty of material in the pipe roll which might be relevant for those researching a particular place or family. The problem is finding it. The roll is about as long as *Moby Dick*, so it would be futile to read all the way through it in the hope of stumbling upon a particular name. If the roll was published with an index of people and places, then all would be made plain. Such an index would contain more than 19,000 individual references to entries in the roll. Until that is available, the local and family historian faces a laborious task, even if they know which county to examine, and roughly what year to begin. In the case of a fine or amercement from a particular fine roll or court roll, for instance, the place to start looking would be the *Nova oblata* of the appropriate county for that year, or at least within the following few years. But the information in the roll seldom stands by itself. The roll records money that is owed and money that is paid, with brief descriptions of the people involved and the reason for the transaction. This usually has to be taken together with other sources to build up a fuller picture, but the pipe roll can contribute important details. A couple of examples may illustrate what can be found, and how it has to be read in conjunction with other records.

The Lincolnshire *Nova oblata* in the 1259 roll include a brief entry recording that John de Haya had paid into the Treasury 10*m.* of silver for 1*m.* of gold, for having the king's licence to contract a certain marriage (1484). As this was in the *Nova oblata*, it was evidently a new transaction. In addition, as John had already paid, it would not need to be copied into the following year's roll – it was over and done with. It was evidently a fine, and indeed it is to be found in the 1257–58 fine roll. The fine was made in May 1258, just before the Oxford parliament which put an end to Henry III's personal rule. It was recorded as a fine of 1*m.* of gold, to be paid into the Wardrobe, but it was not then copied onto the originalia roll which would have informed the Exchequer about the fine. This was a common practice before the baronial council took over the government; Henry III was trying to build up a stockpile of gold, by having fines paid directly to the Wardrobe, while avoiding the scrutiny of the Exchequer. After the revolution, at the end of 1258, the new regime used the originalia roll to inform the Exchequer about the outstanding fines of gold, including this one, which should now be pursued by the sheriffs and paid to the Treasury. John actually paid his fine in silver, at the conventional exchange rate of ten marks of silver for one of gold, and quite quickly; it was received by the Treasury on 26 May 1259, as 10*m.* 'for having the marriage of the daughters of Walter Ledet'.[29]

The fine roll tells us that the marriage in question had been contracted between John de Haya's two sons and the daughters of Walter Ledet. John de Haya (or de la Haye) was a Lincolnshire knight and a loyal supporter of Simon de Montfort. While Montfort held power in 1264–65, Haya was made steward of the royal household, then constable of Dover castle. Walter Ledet had inherited lands in Northamptonshire from his father Wischard Ledet, including the honours and hundreds of Corby and Chipping Warden. The pipe roll includes Corby in the Northamptonshire *terre date*, showing it as being held by the heir of Wischard Ledet (978). Walter was thus a tenant-in-chief, holding land directly from the king. When Walter died in 1256, he had no sons, and his daughters were minors, putting their marriages (and inheritances) at the king's disposition. The daughters, Alice and Christiana, must have been very young; an inquiry in about 1267 stated that they were then aged 12 and 11, while another in 1271 stated that Christiana, the younger daughter, was aged 15. Walter's widow, Ermintrude, was given custody of Corby until the heirs came of age. Simon de Montfort became involved in 1258, ensuring the ratification of the sale of the girls' marriage to John de Haya. Ermintrude married again, to Robert Peche, who was one of the rebels in the Isle of Ely. After their surrender, Corby was taken into the king's hand, then restored to Ermintrude in 1267. At some point, the arrangement with Haya fell apart. Both he and Peche were very closely associated with the defeated Montfortian cause. Instead, the Ledet daughters were to marry the sons of William le Latimer, the royalist escheator and sheriff of Yorkshire. By 1268, Alice was married to William le Latimer junior, and the Ledet inheritance was divided up. Corby was assigned to Alice and thus passed to her Latimer descendants.[30]

A short reference in the pipe roll thus leads to a complex family saga, and to an explanation of the way in which Corby passed from the Ledets to the Latimers. This slice of family and local history would not be immediately apparent from the pipe roll entry alone. Nor would the pipe roll entry necessarily catch the attention of anyone researching the history of Corby, because it is to be found in the Lincolnshire, rather than Northamptonshire, account. There are some other interesting features: it throws some light on the way in which heiresses were effectively bought and sold, in this case as small children, together with their inheritances; and it is an example of Henry III's attempts to by-pass the Exchequer and accumulate a gold treasure, which was reversed by the reforming government in 1258–59.

Another entry from Lincolnshire illustrates an aspect of the history of families and places, payment for relief, which is frequently to be found in the pipe roll. Relief was a payment by a tenant-in-chief to the king, in order to gain possession of lands which he or she had inherited. Chapter 2 of the 1215 Magna Carta, repeated in 1225, had set the amounts to be paid for relief: for the heir or heirs of an earl or baron £100; for the heir or heirs of a knight, for a whole knight's fee, 100*s*. at most. In this case, Hugh of Swarby paid 25*s*. into the Treasury for his relief (1707). This debt first appeared in the Lincolnshire *Nova oblata* in the 1252–53 pipe roll, then in the *De oblatis* section in 1253–54, and so on until 1259 when it was paid. There is more detail to be found in the fine roll. An entry dated 8 October 1253 records that Hugh of Swarby, son and heir of Robert of Swarby, had done fealty to the king for the lands which his father had held in chief from the king. The escheators (the royal officials who administered land which had come into the king's hands) were to take security from Hugh for him paying 25*s*. for his relief at the Exchequer in January 1254. The escheators were then to give Hugh possession of Robert's lands, which had been taken into the king's hand after Robert's death. This was a routine procedure. There had been an inquisition post-mortem on 12 September 1253, which found that Hugh was Robert's heir, and of full age to inherit. The property in question was in Marton, Lincolnshire, worth £7 a year, and held in chief from the king by service of a quarter of a knight's fee. Robert had held other lands from other lords, but the inquisition was only concerned with this holding in chief. As it was a quarter of a knight's fee, Hugh had to pay a quarter of the usual relief, which he did, even if rather belatedly.[31] Similar entries for payment of relief are to be found throughout the pipe roll, enabling one to track the inheritance of property held directly from the king.

A final example from the 1259 roll illustrates the way in which sheriffs and other local officials used the revenues they collected for expenditure in the counties, at the direction of central government. It also shows how the pipe roll can provide records of building works which might be significant for local history. The list of expenditure by the sheriff of Hampshire includes two sums for works in Winchester castle: £233 14s. 2½d. for panelling the pantry and store-room, removing earth from the ditch under the tower, examining and repairing the walls of the castle, making a postern gate with new timber, and so on; and £280 19s. 8d. for panelling the king's privy chamber, renewing certain pictures, rebuilding the great tower, and much more (3). These improvements to the castle are part of the pattern of works there in the thirteenth century, as a favoured royal residence. During his personal rule, Henry III spent some £8,500 on the castle. The works were largely not to strengthen it, but to make it more comfortable for the king and queen. It was one of the places where they preferred to spend Christmas – Henry celebrated Christmas at Winchester eighteen times in the course of his reign.[32]

For each example of the expenditure shown in the pipe roll, the works are said to be by writ of the king and by view and testimony of two named men. This was the normal procedure for controlling major expenditure on building. The king's writ instructed the sheriff to carry out the work, and after the event he had to produce detailed statements of his expenditure, with expert witnesses to testify that the money had actually been spent, and was a reasonable amount. For the works in Winchester castle, we have the writs recorded in the *liberate* roll, from 29 June and 28 November 1256, setting out the works required. We also have a fragment of the detailed particulars of the first set of works, which goes into such details as the wages of ten labourers at 2d. a day, and of six carpenters making a wooden stair, for one week, 12s. at 2s. a week each. The sheriff recovered his expenditure by setting it against the revenues he had collected locally, in this case the county profit from the past two years (4,5). In addition, further writs to town bailiffs directed other local revenues to be handed to the sheriff for the castle works. These sums, from the farms of Portsmouth, Andover, Winchester, and Basingstoke, are recorded in the pipe roll, together with an acknowledgement of their receipt by the sheriff (39, 74, 116, 172, 466).[33]

The pipe rolls are full of such detail, because the Exchequer wanted to ensure that revenues were collected and spent relatively effectively and honestly. This did not always succeed: there were numerous examples of crooked and cruel sheriffs, who defrauded both the Exchequer and the people of their counties.[34] It was not a coincidence that the villain of the Robin Hood stories was the sheriff of Nottingham. But the efforts to impose accountability on officials meant that written records had to be composed and preserved. The Exchequer clerks inadvertently left to us the evidence, taken from just one pipe roll, which helps to illuminate both the finances of central government and the details of local and family history.

Notes

1 For the events of that year, and the reasons for the baronial coup, see Adrian Jobson, *The First English Revolution: Simon de Montfort, Henry III and the Barons' War* (London: Continuum, 2012).
2 The thesis and transcription can be downloaded from the British Library: https://ethos.bl.uk/OrderDetails.do?uin=uk.bl.ethos.628093, or from King's College London: https://kclpure.kcl.ac.uk/portal/files/12504736/Studentthesis-Richard_Cassidy_2012.pdf. The photographs of the roll are on the AALT website: http://aalt.law.uh.edu/PipeTC/PR103tc.html.
3 For instance, Victor E. Watts, *The Cambridge Dictionary of English Place-names: based on the collections of the English Place-Name Society* (Cambridge: Cambridge University Press, 2004). An older dictionary has the advantage of referring to the traditional counties: Eilert Ekwall, *The Concise Oxford Dictionary of English Place-names*, 4th ed. (Oxford: Clarendon Press, 1960). See also the website: "Survey of English Place-Names," https://epns.nottingham.ac.uk.
4 TNA: E 372/101 rot. 13 [image 1383].
5 Johnson and Jenkinson, *English Court Hand*, Part I, 148.
6 TNA: E 372/110 rot. 3 [image 9351].
7 Northamptonshire sheriff's account 1258–59, TNA: E 389/105.
8 Kent TNA: E 389/79–80 m. 10; Berkshire E 389/46 rot. 2; Northumberland E 101/505/10 m. 1; Nottinghamshire TNA: E 389/123 m. 4d; Somerset E 389/128 m. 1.
9 *Calendar of the Fine Rolls*, and supporting information, are available at "Henry III Fine Rolls Project," https://finerollshenry3.org.uk/home.html. For more detail about the fine and originalia rolls, see on that site: David Carpenter, 'Introduction to Rolls', and Paul Dryburgh, 'Originalia Rolls'.
10 *CFR*, 1257–58, no. 835.
11 *CFR*, 1258–59, nos. 216, 657. De Lisle's attermed debt first appears in the next pipe roll, TNA: E 372/104 rot. 18 [image 1926].
12 David Crook, *Records of the General Eyre*, PRO Handbooks, (London: HMSO, 1982), 109, 119.
13 Andrew H. Hershey, *Special Eyre Rolls of Hugh Bigod, 1258–1260*, 2 vols. (London: Selden Society, 2021), no. 315.
14 C.A.F. Meekings, *Crown Pleas of the Wiltshire Eyre, 1249* (Devizes: Wiltshire Archaeological and Natural History Society, 1961), 106–15.
15 For the sake of simplicity, references below are solely to the King's Remembrancer's memoranda rolls, TNA: E 159/32 and 33. The corresponding Lord Treasurer's rolls are TNA: E 368/34 and 35.
16 TNA: E 159/32 m. 3 [image 0005]. R. F. Treharne and I. J. Sanders, *Documents of the Baronial Movement of Reform and Rebellion, 1258–1267* (Oxford: Clarendon Press, 1973), 118–23. *CFR*, 1257–58, nos. 178–80.
17 TNA: E 159/32 m. 5 [image 0012] (appointment), 2 [image 0004] (oath), 5d [image 0097] (summons). TNA: E 401/39 m. 8–10 (receipts).
18 TNA: E 159/32 m. 19 [image 0052] (adventus), 19d [image 0138] (view).

19 TNA: E 159/33 m. 27 [image 0061] (adventus); E 401/41 m. 1, 4 (receipts).
20 TNA: E 159/33 m. 27d [image 0120] (dies dati).
21 TNA: E 401/41 m. 9.
22 TNA: E 401/60 m. 1; E 401/40 m. 1.
23 TNA: E 401/40 m. 2; E 401/41 m. 4; E 401/42 m. 8.
24 TNA: E 401/40 m. 6; E 401/41 m.1.
25 TNA: E 159/33 m. 26 [image 0059].
26 TNA: E 401/44 m. 11 (receipt). TNA: E 159/33 m. 14 [image 0031] (Cumberland account). It would seem that debtors were actually imprisoned: a few years earlier, there was a complaint that sheriffs and others arrested while accounting at the Exchequer were being sent to the Fleet prison (TNA: E 368/29 m. 14 [image 4870]).
27 Bruce M.S. Campbell, "Global climates, the 1257 mega-eruption of Samalas volcano, Indonesia, and the English food crisis of 1258," *TRHS* 27, 6th Series (2017). Matthew Paris, *Chronica Majora*, 7 vols., ed. Henry Richards Luard, Rolls Series (London: Longman, 1872–83), V, 290.
28 Noël Denholm-Young, *Richard of Cornwall* (Oxford: Basil Blackwell, 1947), 97–8. David Carpenter, "The meetings of kings Henry III and Louis IX," *Thirteenth Century England* 10 (2005): 8.
29 *CFR*, 1257–58, nos. 694, 1,257. TNA: E 401/40 m. 6.
30 John Robert Maddicott, *Simon de Montfort* (Cambridge: Cambridge University Press, 1994), 66–8. Ledet family tree in Helen M. Cam, *Liberties and Communities in Medieval England* (London: Merlin Press, 1963), 125–6. Descent of Chipping Warden in I.J. Sanders, *English Baronies: A Study of their Origin and Descent 1086–1327* (Oxford: Clarendon Press, 1960), 33–4. *Calendar of Inquisitions Post Mortem and Other Analogous Documents Preserved in the Public Record Office*, 26 vols. (London: HMSO, 1904–2010), I Henry III, nos. 916, 781. *Calendar of the Patent Rolls*, 1247–58, 529, 631. *Calendar of the Patent Rolls*, 1266–72, 374. *Close Rolls of the Reign of Henry III, Preserved In the Public Record Office*, 14 vols. (London: HMSO, 1902–1938), 1256–59, 4, 34. *Close Rolls Henry III*, 1264–68, 348, 545–6. Mark Page and Matthew Bristow, eds., *A History of the County of Northampton. Volume VII, Corby and Great Oakley*, Victoria County History (London: Published for the Institute of Historical Research by Boydell & Brewer, 2013), 28–9. Helen M. Jewell, "Latimer, William, first Lord Latimer (d. 1304), baron and soldier," *ODNB*, www.oxforddnb.com/view/10.1093/ref:odnb/9780198614128.001.0001/odnb-9780198614128-e-16101.
31 Carpenter, *Magna Carta*, 39, 468. TNA: E 372/97 rot. 17d [image 1317]; E 372/98 rot. 15d [image 8330]. *CFR*, 1252–53, no. 347. *Calendar of Inquisitions Post Mortem*, I Henry III, no. 271. *Liber Feodorum: The Book of Fees, Commonly Called Testa de Nevill*, 3 vols. (London: HMSO, 1920–31), 1031, 68.
32 Brown, Colvin and Taylor, *History of the King's Works: The Middle Ages*, II, 859–62. Derek Keene, *Survey of Medieval Winchester*, 2 vols., Winchester Studies, (Oxford: Clarendon Press, 1985), 103.
33 *Calendar of the Liberate Rolls Preserved in the Public Record Office*, 6 vols. (London: HMSO, 1916–1964), IV 1251–60, 307, 343, 428, 436. Howard Montagu Colvin, ed., *Building Accounts of King Henry III* (Oxford: Clarendon Press, 1971), 185–7.
34 For example, Richard Cassidy, "William Heron, 'Hammer of the Poor, Persecutor of the Religious', Sheriff of Northumberland, 1246–58," *Northern History* 50, 1 (2013).

5 Pipe rolls in the thirteenth century

Although the physical appearance of pipe rolls changed little in the course of the thirteenth century, there were major changes to their contents. These changes pulled in opposite directions, one making the rolls longer, the others making them shorter. An important innovation, adding much more content, was the introduction of the foreign accounts as a separate section. These accounts, an addition to the traditional sheriffs' accounts for the counties, grew over the course of the century. On the other hand, the Exchequer made repeated attempts to trim the size of the county accounts. This was done by reducing the amount of new material recorded in the county accounts each year, and by cutting out old material which would otherwise have been copied from one year to the next. Despite the apparent conservatism of the Exchequer, it did have these occasional fits of innovation. It was also careful to conserve its records, not simply as archives for their own sake, but as working documents. Another aspect of the role of pipe rolls over the century is demonstrated by the internal evidence of their use: the rolls were not simply compiled and stored away but were consulted and cross-referenced over many years.

Too much information

From the very beginning of the thirteenth century, the Exchequer was faced with the problem of having to record masses of information about a large number of small transactions. As an example, take the results of the eyre of 1198–99, when a group of justices led by Hugh Bardolf visited Lincolnshire, Nottinghamshire and Derbyshire, and Yorkshire. This produced a flood of amercements. In the 1200 pipe roll, all three county entries recorded that their sheriffs accounted for lump sums for amercements of men and vills; their names, debts, and reasons for their debts were annotated in the roll which the justices had delivered to the Treasury. In other words, the number of payments was already too large to be copied out in the pipe roll, and the details were left in the roll produced by the justices. In the case of Yorkshire, the sheriff accounted for £641, delivered to the Treasury in 972 tallies. The tallies still had to be cut, but at least the list of payments did not have to be copied. Many debts were still outstanding, however, and a long list of these appeared in the pipe roll. Many of these entries were at some point marked with the letter *t* or a cross, +. These markings are explained in the following years' pipe rolls. In 1201, the sheriff accounted for the amercements of those whose names were marked in the preceding roll with a letter *t* as a sign that they were quit. In 1202, the roll has a heading referring to those who were marked with a cross (*cruisiati*) in the preceding roll. The Exchequer clerks thus escaped having to write out again the names of the debtors, when they paid their debts. The need to avoid too much detail in the pipe rolls was similarly demonstrated following the eyre's next visit to Yorkshire in 1202; the 1203 roll records that the sheriff accounted for £925 in 1,138 tallies.[1]

The Exchequer clerks had two problems, shown in these examples from the beginning of the century. One was to avoid over-loading the rolls with a mass of relatively trivial new entries, like these Yorkshire cases of about a thousand amercements averaging less than £1 each. They could be left on the rolls produced by the justices, with the sheriff accounting for a lump sum on behalf of the debtors. The other was to minimize the amount of information in old entries having to be copied from one roll to the next, year after year. In the Yorkshire example, this was achieved by referring back to the original list of debts, when they were paid in subsequent years. As the century progressed, more elaborate devices were introduced to deal with these problems. It is worth explaining them in detail, to make sense of some annotations which readers will find in the pipe rolls. These are not really self-explanatory, and they show how the rolls remained in active use over many years.

Reducing new entries

The essential device for limiting the amount of new material entering the pipe rolls was to leave the detailed information on other rolls and to mark up those rolls as debts were pursued and paid. The other innovation which made the Exchequer's task easier was the dividend tally, introduced in about 1206.[2] Rather than cutting hundreds of tallies as receipts for the individual amounts making up the lump sum paid in by the sheriff, the Exchequer just gave the sheriff a single tally for the whole amount. The lump sum and dividend tally were not necessarily applied to all instances of multiple debts collected by the sheriffs, but they became increasingly common in the pipe rolls, particularly for judicial amercements.

The pipe rolls contain numerous entries following this pattern: *Debita* or *Debita et libertates . . . non sunt in rotulo*. They stand out because they are written in a smaller hand than most of the entries, about two lines of writing for each ruled line, and are placed towards the right margin of the roll. These entries concern the debts for amercements or other impositions relating to a particular court or judicial visitation, such as the eyre. When they mention liberties, they also relate to the debts to be collected in liberties outside the sheriff's control. They show that these debts have not been copied individually into the pipe roll, but remain in the lists of amercements and so on which were drawn up by the courts, and forwarded to the Exchequer. These lists were known as estreats. The Exchequer saved itself the labour of copying out long lists of debts by keeping these estreats as its record of what was owed, and marking up the estreats with payments as they were collected. The pipe roll recorded only the lump sums covering the total amounts paid in by the sheriffs, or by the officials of liberties. These *Debita et libertates* entries simply serve as reminders that the full details of the debts have not been included in the pipe roll.

The estreats produced by the courts and sent to the Exchequer could contain hundreds of entries, as we have seen. The Exchequer developed a system of marking up the estreats. Some debts were copied into the pipe rolls, in which case the entry in the estreat was marked *In rotulo*. The remaining debts were marked in the margin of the estreat with the letters: *d*, for debts still owing; *p*, for partial payments; and *t*, for total payment, meaning that the debtor was quit. This was elaborated when debts were summoned more than once. If an entry had originally been marked *d*, each time it was summoned the estreat was marked with a dot above the *d*. When it was finally paid, a *t* was added, and the pipe roll could record that the sheriff had paid in an amount for those whose names were marked with a letter *t* and a letter *d* with so many dots above it. This saved a lot of effort. After the eyre of 1276 in London, the sheriff was sent a summons containing nearly 700 fines and amercements. Rather than copying them all into the pipe roll, the 1277 roll merely records: 'Amercements before Master Roger de Seyton and his colleagues at the Tower of London. The sheriffs account for £137 3*s*. 4*d*. from the amercements of men before whose names is placed a letter *t* in the roll of that eyre'.[3] It is not usually possible to match the pipe roll entries with the estreats, because few estreats survive. In 1316 Edward II pardoned all the amercements imposed before 1291, and all such amercements shown in the rolls were to be cancelled. Any other information contained in the estreats was copied into new compendium rolls, and the old estreats no longer needed to be preserved.[4]

The Exchequer adopted a similar approach to reducing the amount of material copied into the pipe rolls from the originalia rolls. The originalia rolls were used to convey information from the Chancery to the Exchequer, particularly about the debts owed for fines. The Exchequer would then include details of the fines in the summons sent to sheriffs, who were responsible for collecting these debts. The debts were usually copied into the *Nova oblata* section of the pipe rolls as well. As each entry from the originalia roll was processed by the Exchequer, it would be marked *S'*, to show that it was in the summons, then *In R'*, for *In rotulo*, to show that it was in the pipe roll.[5] Some entries in the originalia rolls of the 1250s and 1260s were marked to show that the debts had been summoned, but not entered into the pipe roll. In a few cases, they were marked instead with the letters *t* and *d*, just like the estreats, and in the 1270s the pipe rolls include entries showing that sheriffs accounted for lump sums from people or communities whose names were marked with a *t* in a particular originalia roll. Many counties in the 1276 pipe roll begin the *Nova oblata* section with such statements, referring to the originalia rolls of the preceding three years.[6]

Reducing old entries

Despite these attempts to keep new debts on the rolls which were sent to the Exchequer, rather than copying them into the pipe rolls, new material was added every year, and then it had to be copied into the following years' rolls so long as it remained unpaid. We have already seen one way of reducing the clutter in the pipe rolls: going back to the previous year's pipe roll, then marking debts which have been paid with a *t*, and in the current year simply recording that the sheriff paid a lump sum for all those debts marked with a *t*. This device is found very frequently in the pipe rolls and helped to reduce the number of entries which had to be copied from one year's pipe roll to the next. It still left the Exchequer clerks with the task of copying unpaid debts year after year. Some such debts were left unpaid for decades, and it must eventually have become clear that they were unlikely ever to be collected. The Exchequer therefore adopted a series of measures to deal with these desperate debts (desperate meaning that there was no hope of payment). These efforts left traces in the pipe rolls, which at first sight may seem rather enigmatic.[7]

There was evidently an attempt to remove such debts in John's reign. In the 1202 pipe roll, many entries are marked with a ø symbol. In the short account for Lancashire, there are thirteen such entries, including two in the *Nova oblata* (which can hardly have been so old as to be beyond hope of collection). None of these debts appears to have been copied into the 1203 roll, where again many entries are marked with ø.[8] This exercise made little impact on the size of the rolls, with removals balanced by new debts being added, so that the rolls for 1202, 1203, and 1204 were all twenty rotulets long.

The next wave of de-cluttering affected the pipe rolls of 1240 and 1241. In the 1240 pipe roll, for example, several entries in the Herefordshire account have written above them *Sed resp' in pullo*; literally, but he answers in the offshoot (*pullus* can mean a young animal, or new growth in a plant). Those entries were copied into a separate roll, the *rotulus pullorum*, but not into succeeding years' pipe rolls. The *rotulus pullorum* still exists, as TNA: E 372/2/20, fifteen rotulets of the same size as pipe roll rotulets, produced in duplicate from time to time over forty years, and at some point gathered together. This roll contains the offshoots from pipe rolls which were extracted in several campaigns to cut out debts which were not worth copying year after year.[9] In the 1257 roll, entries in several counties (Devon, Hampshire, Nottinghamshire, Warwickshire) have been marked with the note *in pullo* written above them. This has also been done in the 1258 roll, for Berkshire, Lincolnshire, London, Norfolk, Northamptonshire, Oxfordshire, Surrey, and Sussex. In the relatively small account for Berkshire, some 108 entries were marked *in pullo*, in London only three. This produced a slimmed-down list of debts to be entered into the next pipe roll covering these counties, the roll for 1259.[10] This exercise was repeated at intervals, and the *rotulus pullorum* includes entries taken from the pipe rolls for 1260 and 1261, then from 1273, 1277, and 1278, as well as a series of debts from Norfolk and Suffolk only, from 1261, 1277, and 1281.

It is not clear why some debts were chosen for removal from the pipe rolls into the *rotulus pullorum*, and not others. They were not necessarily the oldest and presumably most hopeless debts: the Oxfordshire account in the 1260 pipe roll has twenty-three entries marked *in pullo*, of which the oldest date back to 1247 and the latest had first appeared in the previous year.[11] It is also unclear why some counties were left out and others pruned twice in quick succession, in the 1258 and 1260 rolls. The Exchequer had not necessarily given up all hope of recovering these debts: the Essex account in the 1261 pipe roll includes a note indicating that debts *in pullo* should be summoned: *Debita contenta in pullo summoneantur*. A few such debts were eventually paid: two from 1260 and 1261 were noted as having been paid in 1278.[12] But the main intent of the exercise was simply to keep the pipe rolls to a manageable size.

The Exchequer tried another approach to avoiding the time and effort of copying old debts with the Pipe Roll Order of 1270.[13] This sets out the order in which entries should appear in the pipe rolls, first the *corpus comitatus*, then the fixed alms, and so on. It then decrees that the sheriff of each county should be asked to state which entries in the current pipe roll refer to outstanding debts; these debts will be marked *d* in that pipe roll; they will not be repeated in later pipe rolls, but they will be included in the summons sent to the sheriff, and a note about them included at the end of each year's account, until they are paid. This order was put into effect in the next pipe roll account for each county. Taking Somerset and Dorset as an example, its account for 1269–70 was the first to be audited after the order took effect. In the pipe roll for 1270, at the end of the Somerset account, there is a note:

> The debts of various people above whose names the letter *d* is placed in roll 52 [the roll for 1268, the 52nd regnal year], are to be demanded each year. And those for which the sheriff pays nothing are to be summoned when the account has been finished, and the summons sent to the sheriff with the other summonses, as has been provided by the king and his council, as is contained in his letters patent which are in the treasury.[14]

Turning to the 1268 roll, we find that numerous entries have indeed been marked with a *d*. The same was true for each of the counties: debts in the last account before 1270 were marked up with *d*, and at the end of each account from 1270 onwards there was a note similar to the one above. The exercise was repeated in the 1272 pipe roll, where debts were again marked with a *d*, so that they need not be re-copied into the following years' pipe rolls, but would be included in the summons sent to the sheriff each year. The pipe rolls show that this process did sometimes produce results. The 1268 Somerset account has a number of examples of debts marked *d* which have had further notes added in later years, showing that they have been paid. They refer to rolls as far ahead as roll 16 of king Edward, which would be 1288, showing that debts were being summoned and collected, and the marked-up 1268 roll was being updated, for at least twenty years. It is possible to find corresponding references in these later rolls. In our Somerset example, in the 1268 roll, there is an entry for Robert Chantemerle, who owes half a mark because he did not come (to court). This entry is marked *d*, and 'But the sheriff answers in the fifth roll of king Edward'. Turning to that roll, the roll for 1277, we find in the Somerset account the heading: 'Concerning those above whose names is placed the letter *d* in rolls 52 and 56 of king Henry [1268 and 1272]'. Beneath, the sheriff answers for a list of debts, including half a mark from Robert Chantemerle.[15]

The most radical attempt to cut clutter from the pipe rolls followed in 1284, as part of a decree intended to improve Exchequer procedures for the collection of debts, known as the 'statute of Rhuddlan'.[16] One of its provisions was that the initial section of each county's pipe roll account, the *corpus*, should be copied into a separate roll, and need not be repeated year after year in pipe rolls from then on. This measure recognized that the *corpus* – the county farm and the *terre date* deducted from it – stayed the same year after year. There was no point in copying it out into each successive roll, when the only significant detail was the net amount which the sheriff owed after the routine deductions from the farm. The statute also provided for 'dead' farms and desperate debts to be similarly copied into a separate roll, rather than being re-copied over and over again in the pipe rolls. The sheriff could then be asked each year whether any payments had been made, by reference to this separate roll. All this was put into effect by the creation of the new roll, known as the *rotulus de corporibus* (now TNA: E 372/129), containing the material to be excluded from the pipe rolls from then on. This system lasted until 1299, when the *corpus* returned to the pipe rolls for several years, but it was then removed again. A further change took place in 1323, when yet another set of rolls was created for recording desperate debts which had been cut out of the pipe rolls. These rolls, known as the exannual rolls, survive as TNA series E 363.[17]

The effect of the statute of Rhuddlan can best be seen by the example of one county, such as Northamptonshire. The old system was last used in the 1283 pipe roll, in which the county account begins with the *corpus*. This records that the sheriff owes £230 blanch for the farm of the county, then lists the *terre date*, such as £14 in Apthorp for which the men of the town answer. After these deductions, the sheriff would owe a net farm of £4. This *corpus* occupies six lines of text. Following the introduction of the statute, the farm and the *terre date* were copied into the *rotulus de corporibus*, under the heading '*Corpus* of the county of Northampton as contained in roll 11 of king Edward [the 1283 pipe roll]'. In the next pipe roll, for 1284, the Northamptonshire account begins with a heading explaining what has been done: 'The *corpus* of this county is not recorded here, but recorded in a certain roll in which are written all the *corpora* of the counties of England'. It then states that the sheriff owes £4 for the remainder of the county farm after the *terre date*, as shown in the 1283 roll and in preceding rolls, and goes on to the rest of the county account. This became the pattern in subsequent years, with the county account headed by a brief statement that the *corpus* of the county was recorded in the *rotulus de corporibus*, then the first entry, showing that the sheriff owed £4 for the remainder of the county farm after the *terre date*.[18]

The statute also provided for the removal of debts from the pipe roll, so that they need not be copied repeatedly. A number of debts were marked up in the 1283 pipe roll with the comment 'But he answers in the *rotulus de corporibus*'. They were recorded in the *rotulus*, beneath the *corpus*: for example, the 1283 roll includes a debt of 40*d*. for Simon de Fordingeye; this debt was copied into the *rotulus de corporibus*, and thus need not appear in later pipe rolls. As this example shows, the debts removed were often quite trivial. Further debts were copied into the *rotulus de corporibus* from time to time, with new rotulets added to accommodate this growth. The Northamptonshire entries include debts taken from pipe rolls as late as 1317, showing that the *rotulus de corporibus* was in active use for over thirty years.[19]

Pipe rolls and other rolls

The preceding sections have shown that pipe rolls did not stand alone. They were part of a system, involving numerous other rolls, only some of which survive. The memoranda rolls recorded the arrangements for auditing the accounts of each county, and the instructions given to the sheriffs as a result of the audit. The estreats and originalia rolls conveyed information about debts to the Exchequer, which had the task of collecting them; these rolls were then increasingly used as supplements to the pipe rolls, listing the details of individual debts which did not need to be copied into the pipe rolls; the pipe rolls themselves needed only to record the payment of lump sums. The sheriffs had to produce particulars setting out the minutiae of the revenues they collected and spent, to support the summarized statements which appear in the county accounts. The same was true for the officials responsible for the activities which appear in the foreign accounts.

Other types of roll also refer back to old pipe rolls as evidence of debts and payments. The 1233 memoranda roll, for example, refers back to an entry in the 1187 pipe roll. The 1259 memoranda roll orders the distraint of the bishop of Salisbury, for debts contained in the 1239 pipe roll.[20] The pipe roll was the authoritative record, to be brought out and consulted long after it was written. It was therefore cited in court cases, as evidence of transactions many years ago. The Exchequer itself acted as a court, the Exchequer of Pleas. In a 1237 case about tax collected by the sheriff of Berkshire, but not paid into the Exchequer, the court inspected the county's accounts for 1231 and 1232. Such examinations of the rolls could reach much further back. In a 1291 case about the liabilities of the citizens of London, the Exchequer of Pleas referred to evidence from the 1252 pipe roll. The citizens were involved in another case, heard by the king's council in 1255; their liability to pay tallage was demonstrated by citing rolls from 1214, 1223, 1241, 1245, 1249, and 1252.[21]

This demonstrates that, when pipe rolls were complete, at the end of the Exchequer's annual routine of auditing and recording, they were not simply filed and forgotten. They remained in use, as evidence of debts owing and payments made, to be consulted and annotated for many years to come. In the short term, a pipe roll could be marked up to show the outstanding debts which had been collected since it was first written, to save the effort of writing the details all over again into a subsequent roll. In the longer term, the information in the rolls was used when the Exchequer moved to collect outstanding debts. Many debts appear in the pipe rolls as brief statements of the amount owed, with the addition: 'as is contained in roll so-and-so' (*sicut continetur in rotulo* . . .). Following these indications to the earlier roll often leads to a fuller statement of the reason for the debt, or to the process of consolidating several debts into a single sum. Such links to past rolls could extend for several decades into the past: the 1259 pipe roll, for example, includes references to rolls as far back as 1200. And the 1259 roll itself was consulted and used for at least twenty years; it includes an added note, referring to the 1279 roll, to explain what happened to a surplus owed to the earl of Warwick.[22] The Exchequer's work could evidently involve consulting and marking up rolls from long ago, resulting in the annotations which readers can still use to trace debts from one roll to another.

The most methodical and far-reaching exercise in re-visiting old pipe rolls took place in the reign of Edward II. This was part of a concerted effort to raise money from old and neglected debts, and, yet again, to reduce the size of the pipe rolls; they were said in 1323 to be three or four times the size they had been in Edward I's reign. The Exchequer drew up compendium rolls, gathering together all the sums still owing from estreats, going back to the reign of Henry III. These debts were then included in summonses sent to the sheriffs. One such summons, from 1324, ordered the sheriff of Surrey and Sussex to levy nearly a thousand debts, some originating as far back as the 1229 Surrey eyre.[23] Records were sorted and indexed, and a new version of the *rotulus de corporibus* was drawn up. Old pipe rolls were scoured for evidence of outstanding debts. Although falling outside our thirteenth-century confines, this campaign left numerous traces in the thirteenth-century rolls. For example, the 1226 pipe roll includes a note about the burgesses of Gloucester answering for a debt of 100*s*. in the 1325 roll; this note was evidently added a century after the roll was first written, and matches up with an entry in the 1325 roll (which itself refers back to the 1226 roll). The same process of retrospective debt-collecting was applied to the foreign accounts. An account for the administrator of the bishopric of Bath and Wells, during a vacancy in 1264, was marked up to show that he too answered in the 1325 pipe roll. In the 1325 roll, there is the same debt, presumably to be sought from his heirs, some sixty years later.[24] Much of this activity is associated with Edward II's treasurer, Walter Stapeldon, bishop of Exeter. He made himself so unpopular that, when Edward II's regime crumbled in 1326, he was attacked by a mob in London, and beheaded with a bread-knife.[25]

For our purposes, however, Stapeldon's work demonstrates again the significance of the pipe rolls. They were authoritative statements of debts and payments, to be checked and consulted over many years. They were written by, and intended for the use of, the clerks of the Exchequer, and could therefore be written in an abbreviated, formulaic style. At the time, this would have been clear to those familiar with Exchequer usages, but now needs some explanation. Once the reader has become familiar with the conventions, the pipe rolls open up insights into every aspect of government finance and administration. They link to the work of the sheriffs in the counties, to the penalties imposed by the courts, to the fines paid for favours and privileges, and to the management of activities ranging from the royal household to the forests. The Exchequer needed to collect the cash which all these aspects of government produced, and to control how it was spent. The pipe rolls stood at the pinnacle of a pyramid of parchment, summarizing detailed particulars provided by the officials of the administration, and attempting to keep track of debts over many decades. They are initially daunting, not least through their sheer size. Learning how pipe rolls work can be laborious, but the information they contain makes the effort worthwhile.

Notes

1 Crook, *Records of the General Eyre*, 59, 64. Doris Mary Stenton, ed., *The Great Roll of the Pipe for the Second Year of the reign of King John, Michaelmas1200*, NS 12 (London: Pipe Roll Society, 1934), 17, 85, 111–8. Doris Mary Stenton, ed., *The Great Roll of the Pipe for the Third Year of the reign of King John: Michaelmas 1201*, NS 14 (London: Pipe Roll Society, 1936), 152. Doris Mary Stenton, ed., *The Great Roll of the Pipe for the Fourth Year of the Reign of King John: Michaelmas 1202*, NS 15 (London: Pipe Roll Society, 1937), 63. Doris Mary Stenton, ed., *The Great Roll of the Pipe for the Fifth Year of the Reign of King John: Michaelmas 1203*, NS 16 (London: Pipe Roll Society, 1938), 216.
2 Mills, "Experiments in Exchequer Procedure": 156–7.
3 Martin Weinbaum, ed., *The London eyre of 1276* (London: London Record Society, 1976), 525–786. TNA: E 372/121 rot. 18d [image 7189].
4 TNA: E 159/90 m. 11 [image 0024].
5 Paul Dryburgh, "The Form and Function of the Originalia Rolls," In *The Growth of Royal Government Under Henry III*, edited by David Crook and Louise J. Wilkinson (Woodbridge: Boydell Press, 2015), 31. Paul Dryburgh, "Originalia Rolls, 11 and 17 Henry III," In *Calendar of the Fine Rolls of the Reign of Henry*

III, vol. II: 1224–34, edited by Paul Dryburgh and Beth Hartland (Woodbridge: Boydell Press, 2007), xiii, xvii–xix.
6 *CFR 1268–69*, nos. 443–5, 445, 447, 450–2, etc. TNA: E 372/120 rots. 21d, 19d, 1d, 1, for Berkshire, Cambridgeshire, Cumberland, Devon, and so on.
7 The following section draws extensively on the only in-depth study of this topic, Meekings, "Pipe Roll Order."
8 Stenton, *Pipe Roll 1202*, 159–65. Stenton, *Pipe Roll 1203*, 228–34. Also noted in the introduction to this roll, xvii.
9 The Herefordshire account is TNA: E 372/84 rot. 11d [image 4973]. The *rotulus pullorum* entry is E 370/2/20 rot. 7. It is possible that there was an earlier roll serving a similar function. There is a reference in the 1219 pipe roll, at the end of a list of amercements imposed by the eyre: *Require residuum huius itineris in pullo* (Harris, *Pipe Roll 1219*, 86.)
10 TNA: E 372/102, rots. 18 and 5. The *rotulus pullorum* for these years does not survive.
11 TNA: E 372/104 rot. 14 [image 1905].
12 TNA: E 372/105 rot. 11 [image 8720]. E 370/2/20 rot. 9d.
13 Meekings, "Pipe Roll Order." The order itself is on the patent roll TNA: C 66/88 m. 22 [image 0216]. It is printed in Hall, ed., *Red Book of the Exchequer*, III, 842. and in Madox, *History and Antiquities*, 2nd ed., II, 170–1.
14 TNA: E 372/114 rot. 18d [image 0879].
15 TNA: E 372/112 rot. 11 [image 0374]; E 372/121 rot. 3d [image 7129].
16 Statute in *Calendar of the Close Rolls Preserved in the Public Record Office, Edward I*, 5 vols. (London: HMSO, 1900–1908), 1279–88, 294–6. Also attached to the 1284 pipe roll, TNA: E 372/128 rot. 1 [image 3115].
17 Order for exannual rolls: Hall, *Red Book of the Exchequer*, III, 854–5.
18 TNA: E 372/127 rot. 13 [image 2987]; E 372/129 rot. 8 [image 3446]; E 372/128 rot. 14d [image 3324]; E 372/130 rot. 12 [image 3637]. See also the second example in Appendix 1, the Oxfordshire account for 1293, which also begins with the statement that the *corpus* is in the *rotulus de corporibus*.
19 TNA: E 372/127 rot. 13 [image 2990]; E 372/129 rot. 8 [image 3446], rot. 11 [image 3460].
20 Reginald Allen Brown, ed., *Memoranda Rolls 16–17 Henry III* (London: HMSO, 1991), no. 2925. TNA: E 159/32 m. 20 [image 0055].
21 Hilary Jenkinson and Beryl E.R. Formoy, eds., *Select Cases in the Exchequer of Pleas*, Selden Society (London: Bernard Quaritch, 1932), nos. 27, 186. TNA: E 368/30 m. 10 [image 4980].
22 TNA: E372/103 rot. 2d [image 1760]. This is one of several later notes shown here, which stand out because they were added in a lighter ink.
23 Meekings, "Pipe Roll Order," 250. Mark Buck, "The Reform of the Exchequer, 1316–26," *English Historical Review* 98, 387 (1983): 250.
24 Gallagher and Boatwright, eds., *1226 Pipe Roll*, xx, 121. Also online, TNA: E 372/70 rot. 7 [image 7021], where the added note stands out because it is in a darker ink. The Bath and Wells account: E 372/108 rot. 15 [image 9166]. The 1325 roll references are E 372/170 rot. 26 [image 1203] and rot. 29d [image 1436].
25 Mark Buck, *Politics, Finance and the Church in the Reign of Edward II*, Cambridge Studies in Medieval Life and Thought (Cambridge: Cambridge University Press, 1983), 220–1. Stapledon's head was then sent to queen Isabella. This may not be strictly relevant, but if you've read this far in a book about pipe rolls, you deserve a little gory diversion.

Appendix 1
Transcription examples

These two brief samples of pipe rolls come from relatively early and late in the thirteenth century. They are each transcribed in Latin, expanding the abbreviations, together with an English translation. They are both from the beginning of the Oxfordshire account, from the pipe rolls for 1237 and 1293. They have been chosen because photographs of these pipe rolls are freely available online. The reader can thus compare this printed version of the text, and the translation, with the text as it appears in the actual roll. They can also see how the style and content of pipe rolls changed in the course of the century.

The first extract is from the 1237 pipe roll, TNA: E 372/81 rot. 10. The photograph can be found at: *http://aalt.law.uh.edu/AALT4/H3/E372no81/aE372no81fronts/IMG_4525.htm*

The second extract is from the 1293 roll, TNA: E 372/138 rot. 3. The photograph is at: *http://aalt.law.uh.edu/AALT4/E1/E372no138/aE372no-138fronts/IMG_1954.htm*

The transcriptions largely follow Pipe Roll Society conventions: abbreviations have been expanded where the reading is certain; place-names have often been left abbreviated, because of the impossibility of knowing what the writer intended as the full form of the name; capital letters have been added where necessary at the beginning of sentences and for proper names, but removed elsewhere; punctuation has been regularized, with stops omitted from around numbers, and added where necessary at the end of sentences; stops within sentences are treated as commas; the conventional abbreviations for money have been used; insertions in the text are shown within parentheses (thus[i]); editorial queries and comments are shown within square brackets; the | sign has been used to mark line ends within long paragraphs.

The translations try to follow the structure of sentences and paragraphs in the original, to make it easy for the reader to compare the Latin and English versions, even if this constraint leads to a rather stilted English text.

Oxfordshire account, 1237 pipe roll

Oxonia

Johannes de Tywe ut custos reddit compotum de ccc et xxvj li. xiij s. v d. bl. de firma comitatus. In thesauro xij li. xiiij s. et vij d. bl.

 Et in terris datis Amaurico de Sancto Amando heredi Walteri de Verdon' xx li. bl. in Blokesham. Et abbatisse de Godestowe c s. bl. in Hedendon'. Et canonicis de Oseneie xij s. bl. ibidem. Et Philippo de | Albynaco lxj li. bl. in Banton' quamdiu R. placuerit. Et canonicis Sagiensibus x li. bl. in Bricholmeston'. Et Engelardo de Cyconiaco lvij li. viij s. bl. in Besenton' quamdiu R. placuerit. Et in medietate | de Blokesham xx li. bl. de quibus compotus debet reddi infra. [gap] Et xiij infirmis Sancti Bartholomei extra Oxon' xix li. xv s. v d.[1] Et in elemosinis constitutis militibus de Templo j m. Et predictis infirmis (ad pannos¦) | lxv s. Et monachis de Bordeleg' c s. in porcaria de Banton'. Et abbati de Oseneye in donis ix s. v d. et ob. in villa Oxon'. Et custodi domorum R. in Oxon' xxx s. et v d. Et monachis de Thame lx s. in Wi | falda. Et canonicis Sancte Frisewithe xlviij s. et vj d. in Oxon'. Et Petronille que fuit uxor Galfridi fleccarii l s. in molendino de Hedendon' quod vocatur Kingesmill'. Et abbati de Oseneye vj s. et iiij d. in Bense | ton'. Et infirmis de Wallingeford' iij s. ibidem. Et capellano de Wudestok' l s. Et abbatisse de Godestowe c. s. in Besenton'. Et Roberto capellano Oxon' l s. de liberatione sua. Et Waltero Foliot xxiij s. et iiij d. in Bensen | ton'. Et ecclesie Sancte Marie ij s. et viij d. in Oxon'. Et Mauricio filio Reginaldi Andegavensis x li. in Bensenton'. Et Thome de Craucumbe capellano ministranti in capella Oxon' l s. sicut continetur in rotulo xviij. Et Ricardo Suward' xlij li. et x s. | in Heddendon' de quibus respondet infra. Et cuidam capellano ministranti in capella R. de Wudestok' ad fontem l s. sicut continetur in rotulo precedenti.

 Et Matildi filie Gilberti de Blokesham iiij li. v s. et iiij d. sicut continetur in rotulo precedenti qui (iiij li. v s. et iiij d.¦) debent ei allocari per unum annum sequentem et non amplius sicut continetur ibidem.

 Et in coopertura aule R. Oxon' emendenda iiij li. vij s. iiij d. et ob. per breve Regis et per visum et testimonium Nicolai cissoris et Willelmi molendinarii. Et in emendatione domorum R. in castro Oxon' c s. Et debet xxiiij li. x s. et ij d. bl. | Qui sunt extensi ad xxv li. xiiij s. viij d. numero. Idem reddit compotum de eodem debitum. In thesauro xx li. Et debet c et xiiij s. et viiij d.

Oxfordshire

John of Tew, as custodian, accounts for £326 13*s*. 5*d*. blanch for the farm of the county. In the Treasury, £12 14*s*. 7*d*. blanch.

 And in the lands which have been given, for Aymer de St. Amand, heir of Walter de Verdun, £20 blanch in Bloxham. And for the abbess of Godstow, 100*s*. blanch in Headington. And for the canons of Osney, 12*s*. blanch in the same place. And for Philip de Aubigny, £61 blanch in Bampton for as long as it pleases the king. And for the canons of Séez, £10 blanch in Brighthampton. And for Engelard de Cigogné, £57 8s. blanch in Benson for as long as it pleases the king. And in half of Bloxham, £20 blanch, for which the account should be given below. [gap] And in fixed alms, to the knights of the Temple, 1 mark.[2] And to thirteen invalids of St. Bartholomew [hospital] outside Oxford, £19 15s. 5d. And to these invalids, for cloths, 65s. And to the monks of Bordesley, 100s. in the pigsty of Bampton. And to the abbot of Osney in gifts, 9s. 5½d. in the town of Oxford. And to the keeper of the king's buildings in Oxford, 30s. 5d. And to the monks of Thame, 60s. in Wyfold. And to the canons of St. Frideswide, 48s. 6d. in Oxford. And to Petronilla widow of Geoffrey the fletcher, 50s. in the mill of Headington called Kingsmill. And to the abbot of Osney, 6s. 4d. in Benson. And to the invalids of Wallingford, 3s. in the same place. And to the chaplain of Woodstock, 50s. And to the abbess of Godstow, 100s. in Benson. And to Robert the chaplain of Oxford, 50s. for his stipend. And to Walter Foliot, 23s. 4d. in Benson. And to the church of St. Mary, 2s. 8d. in Oxford. And to Maurice son of Reginald Angevin, £10 in Benson. And to Thomas of Crowcombe the chaplain serving in the chapel of Oxford, 50s. as shown in roll 18. And to Richard Siward, £42 10s. in Headington for which he answers below. And to a certain chaplain serving in the king's chapel at Woodstock at the well, 50s. as shown in the previous roll.

And to Matilda daughter of Gilbert of Bloxham, £4 5s. 4d. as shown in the previous roll, which £4 5s. 4d. should be allowed to her for one further year, and no more, as shown there.

And for repairing the roof of the king's hall in Oxford, £4 7s. 4½d. by writ of the king, and by view and testimony of Nicholas the tailor and William the miller. And for repair of the king's buildings in Oxford castle, 100s. And he [the sheriff] owes £24 10s. 2d. blanch. Which amounts to £25 14s. 8d. by number. He accounts for that debt. In the Treasury, £20. And he owes 114s. 8d.

Oxfordshire account, 1293 pipe roll

Oxon'

Corpus huius comitatus annotatur in rotulo de corporibus comitatuum sicut continetur in rotulo xij.

Willelmus de Bremmeschete vicecomes reddit compotum de lxj li. xv s. j d. bl. de remanenti firme comitatus post terras datas sicut continetur in rotulo xij. In thesauro nichil. [gap] Et in elemosina constituta militibus de Templo j m. Et priori | et conventui Sancte Frideswyde Oxon' ad sustentacionem unius capellani singulis diebus divina celebrantis in ecclesia predicta in ecclesia predicta[3] in honore Sancte Frideswide, et ad sustentacionem iiij cereorum die noctuque ardentium | circa feretrum eiusdem virgine, x m. Et in liberatione j probatoris per cc lxix dies, j per c iiij^{xx} xix dies, j per lxxiij dies, et unius per c lxviij dies, lix s. j d. Et debet lj li. xix s. vij d. bl. qui sunt extensi ad liiij li. | xj s. vj d. ob. numero. De quibus burgenses ville Oxon' debent respondere de xl li. de firma sua que pertinent ad firmam vicecomitis, et respondent infra. Et debet vicecomes xiiij li. xj s. vj d. ob. Idem reddit compotum de | eodem debitum. In thesauro nichil. Et in superplusagio quod habet infra xiiij li. xj s. vj d. ob. [gap] Et quietus est.

[two lines blank]

ft'[4] Idem vicecomes reddit compotum de c m. de firma pro proficuo huius comitatus et comitatus Berk' sicut continetur in rotulo precedenti. In thesauro iiij^{xx} vj li. j m. per ij tallias. Et habet de superplusagio xx li. qui allocantur ei supra et in Item Berk'.

Burgenses Oxon' reddunt compotum de xl li. de firma sua pro vicecomite sicut supra continetur. [gap] In thesauro liberaverunt. Et quieti sunt.

[one line blank]

ft' Corvesarii Oxon' reddunt compotum de xv s. pro gilda sua et pro j uncia auri. In thesauro xx s. Et habent de superplusagio v s. qui allocantur ei infra.

ft' Idem vicecomes debet xviij d. de ij forgiis in Oxon'. Et viij d. de purpresturis. Et viij d. de Roberto le Mercer. Summa ij s. x d. de quibus ballivus ville Oxon' respondet in Item Berk'.

Heredes Ricardi de Oyly [gap] iiij li. iij s. iiij d. de pluribus auxiliis et scutagiis sicut continetur in rotulo primo. [gap] Heredes Sewalli filii Fucheri [gap] lxx s. de ij debitis contentis in rotulo primo.

[gap] de Hedon'[5] de annis viij, ix et x°, sicut continetur in rotulo xiiij.

ft' Vicecomes [gap] ij m. et dim. de firma domus que fuit Jocei filii Mossy. Et c xvij m. et dim. de eadem de annis preteritis.

Oxfordshire

> The body [*corpus*] of this county is noted in the roll of bodies of the counties, as shown in roll 12.

William of Bramshott, sheriff, accounts for £61 15s. 1d. blanch for the remainder of the farm of the county, after [deduction of] the lands which have been given, as shown in roll 12. In the Treasury, nothing. [gap] And in fixed alms, to the knights of the Temple, 1 mark. And to the prior and convent of St. Frideswide, Oxford, for the maintenance of one chaplain celebrating mass every day in that church in honour of St. Frideswide, and for the maintenance of four candles burning day and night around the shrine of that virgin, 10 marks. And for payment for one approver for 269 days, one for 199 days, one for 73 days, and one for 168 days, 59s. 1d. And he [the sheriff] owes £51 19s. 7d. blanch, which amounts to £54 11s. 6½d. by number. Of which, the burgesses of the town of Oxford should answer for £40 for their farm, which is included in the sheriff's farm, and they answer below. And the sheriff owes

£14 11s. 6½d. He accounts for that debt. In the Treasury, nothing. And in the surplus which he has below, £14 11s. 6½d. [gap] And he is quit.

Done. The same sheriff accounts for 100 marks for the farm of the profit of this county and Berkshire, as shown in the previous roll. In the Treasury, £86 1 mark by two tallies. And he has a surplus of £20, which is allowed to him above and in [the continuation of the account for] Berkshire.

The burgesses of Oxford account for £40 for their farm for the sheriff, as shown above. [gap] They have paid [it] into the Treasury. And they are quit.

Done. The cordwainers of Oxford account for 15s. for their guild and for one ounce of gold. In the Treasury, 20s. And they have a surplus of 5s. which is allowed to them below.

Done. The same sheriff owes 18d. for three forges in Oxford. And 8d. for purprestures. And 8d. for Robert le Mercer. Total 2s. 10d., for which the bailiff of the town of Oxford answers in [the continuation of the account for] Berkshire.

The heirs of Richard de Oyly [gap] £4 3s. 4d. for several aids and scutages as shown in roll 1. [gap] The heirs of Sewal son of Fulcher [gap] 70s. for two debts shown in roll 1.

[gap] for Headington for years 8, 9, and 10, as shown in roll 14.

Done. The sheriff [gap] 2½ marks for the farm of the building which belonged to Josce son of Moses. And 117½ marks for the same for previous years.

Notes

1 There are marks above the line before and after this sentence, to indicate that it should be transposed with the sentence after it.
2 Sentence transposed with the next, as instructed in the original, to make it plain that fixed alms begins here.
3 Phrase repeated in original.
4 This abbreviation before some entries is probably *fecit*, meaning that the sheriff has collected the debt and is answerable for it.
5 In earlier rolls, written as Hedendon'.

Appendix 2
Glossary

adventus The occasion, after Michaelmas and Easter, when sheriffs and representatives of boroughs were expected to appear at the Exchequer, to pay in the revenues of the preceding half-year.

aid A tax imposed on **tenants-in-chief**, linked to the marriage of the king's eldest daughter, or the knighting of his eldest son.

amercement A financial penalty imposed by a court.

attermination An arrangement to pay a debt by instalments.

beaupleder A collective fine imposed at the beginning of a court session, to avoid penalties for procedural errors.

blanched Applied to sums of money in pipe rolls, showing a nominal value that should be increased by one-twentieth to give the amount due in cash terms.

calendar An edition of a record, published as an English summary.

carucage A tax imposed on land, nominally related to the number of ploughs a property could support.

chancellor's roll An approximate duplicate of the pipe roll, produced each year.

Chancery The government department, usually travelling with the king, which dealt with royal correspondence, writing and sealing writs and charters.

compendium rolls Rolls compiled in the reign of Edward II to gather together information about unpaid debts, extracted from earlier **estreats** and pipe rolls.

corpus comitatus The traditional opening section of county accounts in the pipe rolls, showing the county farm, and the amount to be deducted for the *terre date*.

county farm The fixed annual sum which the sheriff agreed to pay as **farmer** for a county. Sheriffs who collected more than that sum could keep the surplus (subject to **increment** and **profit** – see below). The amounts remained unchanged throughout the thirteenth century.

custodian An administrator, such as a sheriff who collected and delivered all the revenues of his county, and was paid a fixed sum in return, as distinct from a **farmer**.

demesne The manors and boroughs owned and administered by the king himself.

desperate debts Debts which the Exchequer had little or no hope of collecting. These were periodically culled from the pipe rolls.

dies dati Days allocated for the audit of sheriffs' accounts.

distraint Action to enforce a debt, by seizure of the debtor's property.

dividend tally A tally stick cut as a receipt for a lump sum payment, representing multiple individual debts.

dorse The reverse side of a membrane or rotulet making up a roll.

escheator An official administering lands which have come into the king's hand, for instance by forfeiture or during the minority of heirs.

estreat A roll listing the financial penalties imposed by a court, sent to the Exchequer, which was then responsible for the collection of these debts.

exannual rolls Rolls compiled from 1323 onwards, listing **desperate debts** which had been removed from the pipe rolls.

exchange The place where foreign coins and silver ingots could be exchanged for English coins. Administered together with the mints which produced the coins.

Exchequer The government department concerned with financial matters. The Upper Exchequer set policy and audited officials' accounts. The Lower Exchequer handled cash, receiving and making payments in coins.

Exchequer of Pleas The judicial aspect of the Exchequer, when it acted as a court.

eyre The court which travelled around the counties, hearing both civil and criminal cases, and investigating royal rights and local abuses. In principle, each county would be visited every seven years or so, to hear the most serious cases which had arisen since the last visit.

farmer A person who undertook to make a fixed annual payment for a county, hundred, manor, and so on, as distinct from a **custodian**.

fine A payment offered to the king in return for a concession or favour. These offers were recorded by the Chancery on the fine rolls.

fixed alms Regular payments from the county farm, made automatically by the sheriff every year, such as the annual payment from each county of one mark to the Templars.

foreign accounts The accounts in the pipe rolls of officials other than the sheriffs; everything except the county accounts, usually gathered together in a section of the pipe roll, known as the *rotuli compotorum*.

hundred An administrative sub-division of a county, which held a regular court; in northern counties, known as a wapentake. Many hundreds were farmed out, or administered by lords' bailiffs rather than sheriffs.

increment A fixed amount over and above the county farm, paid by the sheriffs of a few counties.

issue roll A roll produced in duplicate or triplicate by the Exchequer, recording details of cash paid out, in date order.

liberate roll A roll produced by the Chancery, copying the writs it sent out ordering payments to be made. The Exchequer also kept a liberate roll, copying the writs it received.

liberty An area held from the king with its own privileges, such as a private hundred.

memoranda roll A roll produced each year by the Exchequer, in duplicate, recording anything worthy of official note, including the administrative arrangements for auditing accounts and producing the pipe rolls.

Michaelmas The feast of St Michael, 29 September, which was the last day of the Exchequer's year. The next day, the morrow of Michaelmas, was marked by the **adventus** of the sheriffs, and the beginning of a new term.

Nova oblata The heading of the final section of the county accounts in the pipe rolls, recording new debts which had arisen since the previous roll. Literally, 'new offerings'.

De oblatis The heading of the next-to-last section of each county account, recording the outstanding debts which had first appeared in the preceding roll.

originalia roll A roll in which the Chancery recorded information to be transmitted to the Exchequer, particularly details of fines which were to be collected, but also other material, such as the appointment of sheriffs.

particulars The detailed statement of revenues making up the county farm, which **custodian** sheriffs had to deliver to the Exchequer. Similarly for other officials whose accounts were audited.

profit A sum in addition to the county farm, which sheriffs were expected to produce. For **farmer** sheriffs, this was a fixed sum, set when they took up office. Profits tended to increase, particularly in the 1240s and 1250s.

receipt roll A roll produced by the Exchequer, recording cash paid in. One version showed receipts in date order; another listed payments of lump sums, arranged by county.

record type A nineteenth-century attempt to reproduce in print the symbols indicating abbreviation and contraction used in medieval records. Repulsive.

regnal year The year used to date pipe rolls, etc, counting from the date on which a king's reign was considered to have begun (28 October 1216 for Henry III, 20 November 1272 for Edward I).

relief The payment due from a **tenant-in-chief** in order to take possession of lands which had been inherited.

rotulet A component part of a pipe roll, comprising two parchment membranes stitched together. The rotulets were gathered together, and stitched at the head, to make up a pipe roll.

rotulus de corporibus A roll introduced in 1284 to record the details of the county farms, and of desperate debts, which were extracted from the pipe roll, and thus no longer needed to be copied every year into successive pipe rolls.

rotulus pullorum A roll listing debts extracted from pipe rolls, from time to time; these debts were marked *in pullo* in the pipe roll, and no longer copied into later rolls.

scutage A tax imposed on **tenants-in-chief**, in lieu of military service, based on the number of knights they owed.

summons The instructions sent by the Exchequer to the sheriff, listing the debts which should be collected.

tallage An arbitrary tax imposed by the king on the manors and boroughs of the demesne, and on the Jewish community.

tally A wooden stick in which notches were cut to represent a payment which had been received. The stick was then split, with the payer keeping his half as a receipt.

tenant-in-chief A tenant holding lands directly from the king, and thus liable for knight service.

terre date Literally, 'lands which have been given'; the royal manors and boroughs which were originally administered by the sheriff and contributed to the county farm, but had since been granted away or leased out.

vacancy When a bishop or abbot died, the bishopric or abbey fell into the king's hands, so that the king could appoint an administrator and receive the revenues, until a successor was appointed.

Wardrobe The financial department concerned with the royal household. It travelled with the king, and expanded in times of war to handle military finance.

References

Unprinted primary sources

All unprinted sources are in The National Archives (TNA), Kew, in the following TNA catalogue classes:

C 66	Chancery: Patent rolls
E 36	Treasury of the Receipt: Miscellaneous books
E 101	King's Remembrancer: Accounts various
E 159	King's Remembrancer: Memoranda rolls
E 352	Pipe Office: Chancellor's Rolls
E 364	Pipe Office: Foreign accounts rolls
E 368	Lord Treasurer's Remembrancer: Memoranda rolls
E 370	LTR and Pipe Office: Miscellaneous rolls
E 372	Pipe Office: Pipe rolls
E 389	LTR and Pipe Office: Miscellanea, new series
E 401	Exchequer of Receipt: Receipt rolls
E 403	Exchequer of Receipt: Issue rolls

Photographs of the records in classes C 66, E 159, E 368, and E 372 are available on the Anglo-American Legal Tradition website.

Printed primary sources

Amt, Emilie, and Stephen D. Church, eds. *Richard Fitz Nigel, Dialogus De Scaccario: The Dialogue of the Exchequer; Constitutio Domus Regis: Disposition of the King's Household*. Oxford: Clarendon Press, 2007.

Barnes, Patricia M., ed. *The Great Roll of the Pipe for the 16th Year of the Reign of King John, Michaelmas 1214*. NS [New Series] 35 London: Pipe Roll Society, 1962.

Brown, R. Allen, ed. *Memoranda Rolls 16–17 Henry III*. London: HMSO, 1991.

———, and James Clarke Holt, eds. *Pipe Roll 17 John and Praestita Roll 14–18 John*. NS 37 London: Pipe Roll Society, 1964.

Calendar of Inquisitions Post Mortem and Other Analogous Documents Preserved in the Public Record Office. 26 vols. London: HMSO, 1904–2010.

Calendar of the Close Rolls Preserved in the Public Record Office, Edward I. 5 vols. London: HMSO, 1900–1908.

Calendar of the Fine Rolls, I, Edward I, 1272–1307. London: HMSO, 1911.

Calendar of the Liberate Rolls Preserved in the Public Record Office. 6 vols. London: HMSO, 1916–1964.

Calendar of the Patent Rolls Preserved in the Public Record Office, Henry III. 4 vols. London: HMSO, 1906–1913.

Cannon, Henry Lewin, ed. *The Great Roll of the Pipe for the Twenty-Sixth Year of the Reign of King Henry the Third A.D. 1241–1242*. New Haven: Yale University Press, 1918.

Cazel, Fred A., ed. *Roll of Divers Accounts for the Early Years of the Reign of Henry III*. NS 44 London: Pipe Roll Society, 1982.

Cazel, Fred A., and Annarie P. Cazel, eds. *Rolls of the Fifteenth of the Ninth Year of the Reign of Henry III for Cambridgeshire, Lincolnshire and Wiltshire; and, Rolls of the Fortieth of the Seventeenth Year of the Reign of Henry III for Kent*. NS 45 London: Pipe Roll Society, 1983.

Close Rolls of the Reign of Henry III, Preserved in the Public Record Office. 14 vols. London: HMSO, 1902–1938.

Colvin, Howard Montagu, ed. *Building Accounts of King Henry III*. Oxford: Clarendon Press, 1971.

Dickson, William. "The Pipe Roll of 1st, 2nd, and 3rd of Edward I, with Remarks Thereon, in Continuation of the Series Published by the Rev. John Hodgson." *Archaeologia Aeliana* 1, 4 (1855): 207–60.

———. *The Pipe Roll for the First, Second and Third Years of the Reign of Edward the First for the County of Northumberland* [Includes reproduction of manuscript transcription of Northumberland pipe rolls for 4–12 Edward I]. Newcastle upon Tyne: George Bouchier Richardson, 1854.

Dryburgh, Paul, and Beth Hartland, eds. *Calendar of the Fine Rolls of the Reign of Henry III*. 3 vols. Woodbridge: Boydell Press, 2007–2009.

Gallagher, Eric, and Lesley Boatwright, eds. *The Great Roll of the Pipe for the Tenth Year of the Reign of King Henry III, Michaelmas 1226*. NS 64 Woodbridge: Pipe Roll Society, 2022.

Green, Judith A., ed. *The Great Roll of the Pipe for the Thirty First Year of the Reign of King Henry I, Michaelmas 1130 (Pipe Roll 1)*. NS 57 London: Pipe Roll Society, 2012.

Hall, Hubert, ed. *The Red Book of the Exchequer*. 3 vols (Rolls Series). London: HMSO, 1896.

Hardy, Thomas Duffus, ed. *Rotuli De Oblatis Et Finibus in Turri Londinensi Asservati, Tempore Regis Johannis*. London: Record Commission (Printed by G. Eyre and A. Spottiswoode), 1835.

Harris, Brian E., ed. *The Great Roll of the Pipe for the Fourth Year of the Reign of King Henry III, Michaelmas 1220*. NS 47 London: Pipe Roll Society, 1987.

———, ed. *The Great Roll of the Pipe for the Third Year of the Reign of King Henry III, Michaelmas 1219*. NS 42 London: Pipe Roll Society, 1976.

Hershey, Andrew H. *Special Eyre Rolls of Hugh Bigod, 1258–1260*. Vols. 131 and 133 London: Selden Society, 2021.

Hunter, Joseph, ed. *Fines, Sive Pedes Finium: Sive Finales Concordiae in Curia Domini Regis: Ab Anno Septimo Regni Regis Ricardi I, Ad Annum Decimum Sextum Regis Johannis, A.D. 1195-A.D. 1214*. London: Record Commission, 1835.

———, ed. *Magnum Rotulum Scaccarii Vel Magnum Rotulum Pipae De Anno Tricesimo-Primo Regni Henrici Primi*. London: Record Commission, 1833.

Jenkinson, Hilary, and Beryl E.R. Formoy, eds. *Select Cases in the Exchequer of Pleas*. Vol. 48 London: Selden Society, Bernard Quaritch, 1932.

Jenks, Stuart, ed. *The Enrolled Customs Accounts Part 1*. Vol. 303 Kew: List & Index Society, 2004.

Johnson, Charles, ed. *Dialogus De Scaccario: The Course of the Exchequer by Richard, Son of Nigel*. London: Thomas Nelson & Sons, 1950.

Liber Feodorum: The Book of Fees, Commonly Called Testa De Nevill. 3 vols. London: HMSO, 1920–1931.

Lilburn, A.J. "The Pipe Rolls of Edward I." *Archaeologia Aeliana* 4, 32 (1954): 323–40.

———. "The Pipe Rolls of Edward I – Part II." *Archaeologia Aeliana* 4, 33 (1955): 163–75.

Meekings, Cecil Anthony Francis, ed. *Crown Pleas of the Wiltshire Eyre, 1249*. Devizes: Wiltshire Archaeological and Natural History Society, 1961.

———, ed. *The 1235 Surrey Eyre*. Vol. 31 Guildford: Surrey Record Society, 1979.

Mills, Mabel H., ed. *The Pipe Roll for 1295, Surrey Membrane*. Vol. 21 London: Surrey Record Society, Wm. Dawson & Sons, 1924 (reprinted 1968).

Paris, Matthew. *Chronica Majora* (Rolls Series. Edited by Henry Richards Luard). 7 vols. London: Longman, 1872–1883.

Parker, Francis H.M., ed. *The Pipe Rolls of Cumberland and Westmorland 1222–1260* (Extra Series, vol. 12). Kendal: Cumberland and Westmorland Antiquarian and Archaeological Society, 1905.

Record Commission. *Rotulus Cancellarii, Vel Antigraphum Magni Rotuli Pipæ De Tertio Anno Regni Regis Johannis*. London: Record Commission, 1833.

Society of Antiquaries of Newcastle upon Tyne. *The Pipe-Rolls, or Sheriff's Annual Accounts of the Revenues of the Crown for the Counties of Cumberland, Westmorland, and Durham, During the Reigns of Henry I, Richard I, and John*. Newcastle: Printed by T. and J. Hodgson, 1847.

Stenton, Doris Mary, ed. *The Great Roll of the Pipe for the Fifth Year of the Reign of King John, Michaelmas 1203*. NS 16 London: Pipe Roll Society, 1938.

———, ed. *The Great Roll of the Pipe for the Fourth Year of the Reign of King John, Michaelmas 1202*. NS 15 London: Pipe Roll Society, 1937.

———, ed. *The Great Roll of the Pipe for the Second Year of the Reign of King John, Michaelmas 1200*. NS 12 London: Pipe Roll Society, 1934.

———, ed. *The Great Roll of the Pipe for the Third Year of the Reign of King John, Michaelmas 1201*. NS 14 London: Pipe Roll Society, 1936.

Sweetman, Henry Savage, ed. *Calendar of Documents Relating to Ireland Preserved in Her Majesty's Public Record Office, London*. 5 vols. London: Longman, 1875–1886.

Treharne, Reginald F., and I. J. Sanders. *Documents of the Baronial Movement of Reform and Rebellion, 1258–1267*. Oxford: Clarendon Press, 1973.

Weinbaum, Martin, ed. *The London Eyre of 1276*. Vol. 12 London: London Record Society, 1976.

Wild, Benjamin Linley, ed. *The Wardrobe Accounts of Henry III*. NS 58 London: Pipe Roll Society, 2012.

Secondary sources

Allen, Martin. *Mints and Money in Medieval England*. Cambridge: Cambridge University Press, 2012.

Richard Ashdowne, David Howlett, and Ronald Latham. *Dictionary of Medieval Latin From British Sources*. 3 vols. Oxford: Published for the British Academy by Oxford University Press, 2018.

Barratt, Nick. "Crisis Management: Baronial Reform at the Exchequer." In *Baronial Reform and Revolution in England, 1258–1267*, edited by Adrian Jobson, 56–70. Woodbridge: Boydell Press, 2016.

———. "Finance on a Shoestring: The Exchequer in the Thirteenth Century." In *English Government in the Thirteenth Century*, edited by Adrian Jobson, 71–86. Woodbridge: Boydell Press, 2004.

———. "The Impact of the Loss of Normandy on the English Exchequer: The Pipe Roll Evidence." In *Foundations of Medieval Scholarship: Records Edited in Honour of David Crook*, edited by Paul Brand and Sean Cunningham, 133–40. York: Borthwick Institute, 2008.

Brown, R. Allen, Howard Montagu Colvin, and Alan John Taylor. *The History of the King's Works: The Middle Ages*. 2 vols. London: HMSO, 1963.

Buck, Mark. *Politics, Finance and the Church in the Reign of Edward II. Cambridge Studies in Medieval Life and thought*. Cambridge: Cambridge University Press, 1983.

———. "The Reform of the Exchequer, 1316–1326." *English Historical Review* 98, 387 (1983): 241–60.

Cam, Helen M. *Liberties and Communities in Medieval England*. London: Merlin Press, 1963.

Campbell, Bruce Mortimer Stanley. "Global Climates, the 1257 Mega-Eruption of Samalas Volcano, Indonesia, and the English Food Crisis of 1258." *TRHS* 27 (6th Series) (2017): 87–121.

Carpenter, David. *Magna Carta*. London: Penguin Classics, 2015.

———. "The Meetings of Kings Henry III and Louis IX." In *Thirteenth Century England X*, edited by Michael Prestwich, Richard Britnell and Robin Frame, 1–30. Woodbrige: Boydell Press, 2005.

Cassidy, Richard. "*Recorda Splendidissima*: The Use of Pipe Rolls in the Thirteenth Century." *Historical Research* 85, 227 (2012): 1–12.

———. "William Heron, 'Hammer of the Poor, Persecutor of the Religious', Sheriff of Northumberland, 1246–1258." *Northern History* 50, 1 (2013): 9–19.

Cheney, Christopher Robert, and Michael Jones. *A Handbook of Dates: For Students of British History* (RHS Guides and Handbooks No. 4. Revised ed). Cambridge: Cambridge University Press, 2000.

Crook, David. *Pipe Rolls* (Short Guides to Records No. 39). London: Historical Association, 1994.

———. *Records of the General Eyre* (PRO Handbooks). London: HMSO, 1982.

Denholm-Young, Noël. *Richard of Cornwall*. Oxford: Basil Blackwell, 1947.

———. *Seignorial Administration in England* (Oxford Historical Series). London: Oxford University Press, 1937.

Douglas, David C., and George W. Greenaway, eds. *English Historical Documents. [Vol. 2], 1042–1189* (2nd ed). London: Eyre Methuen, 1981.

Dryburgh, Paul. "Originalia Rolls, 11 and 17 Henry III." In *Calendar of the Fine Rolls of the Reign of Henry III, Vol. II: 1224–1234*, edited by Paul Dryburgh and Beth Hartland, x–xxiv. Woodbridge: Boydell Press, 2008.

———. "The Form and Function of the Originalia Rolls." In *The Growth of Royal Government under Henry III*, edited by David Crook and Louise J. Wilkinson, 30–43. Woodbridge: Boydell Press, 2015.

Ekwall, Eilert. *The Concise Oxford Dictionary of English Place-Names* (4th ed). Oxford: Clarendon Press, 1960.

Green, Judith A. *The Government of England Under Henry I* (1st paperback ed). Cambridge: Cambridge University Press, 1989.

———. "'Praeclarum Et Magnificum Antiquitatis Monumentum': The Earliest Surviving Pipe Roll." *Bulletin of the Institute of Historical Research* 55, 131 (2007): 1–17.

Hagger, Mark. "A Pipe Roll for 25 Henry I." *EHR* CXXII, 495 (2007): 133–40.

———. "Theory and Practice in the Making of Twelfth-Century Pipe Rolls." In *Records, Administration and Aristocratic Society in the Anglo-Norman Realm*, edited by Nicholas Vincent, 45–74. Woodbridge: Boydell Press, 2009.

Harriss, Gerald Leslie. *King, Parliament, and Public Finance in Medieval England to 1369*. Oxford: Clarendon Press, 1975.

Hodgson, John. *A History of Northumberland: In Three Parts*. Newcastle upon Tyne: Printed by Thomas & James Pigg, 1820–1858.

Howell, Margaret. *Regalian Right in Medieval England*. London: Athlone Press, 1962.

Jewell, Helen M. "Latimer, William, First Lord Latimer (d. 1304), Baron and Soldier." *Oxford Dictionary of National Biography*, 2004. www.oxforddnb.com/display/10.1093/ref:odnb/9780198614128.001.0001/odnb-9780198614128-e-16101.

Jobson, Adrian. *The First English Revolution: Simon De Montfort, Henry III and the Barons' War*. London: Continuum, 2012.

Johnson, Charles. "Introduction." In *The Great Roll of the Pipe for the Second Year of the Reign of King Richard the First, Michaelmas 1190*, edited by Doris Mary Stenton. NS 1 London: Pipe Roll Society, 1925.

———, and Hilary Jenkinson. *English Court Hand A.D. 1066 to 1500: Illustrated Chiefly from the Public Records*. 2 vols. Oxford: Clarendon Press, 1915.

Jurkowski, Maureen, Carrie L. Smith, and David Crook. *Lay Taxes in England and Wales 1188–1688* (Public Record Office Handbook). Kew: PRO Publications, 1998.

Keene, Derek. *Survey of Medieval Winchester* (Winchester Studies). 2 vols. Oxford: Clarendon Press, 1985.

Kypta, Ulla. "How to Be an Exchequer Clerk in the Twelfth Century: What the Dialogue of the Exchequer Is Really about." *History* 103 (2018): 199–222.

———. "The Way a Language Changes: How Historical Semantics Helps Us to Understand the Emergence of the English Exchequer." *Contributions to the History of Concepts* 10, 2 (2015): 29–47.

Latham, Ronald Edward. *Revised Medieval Latin Word-List From British and Irish Sources*. London: Published for the British Academy by Oxford University Press, 1980.

Maddicott, John Robert. *Simon De Montfort*. Cambridge: Cambridge University Press, 1994.

———. *The Origins of the English Parliament, 924–1327*. Oxford: Oxford University Press, 2010.

Madox, Thomas. *The History and Antiquities of the Exchequer of the Kings of England, in Two Periods* (1st ed). London: Printed by John Matthews, 1711.

———. *The History and Antiquities of the Exchequer of the Kings of England, in Two Periods* (2nd ed). 2 vols. London: Printed for William Owen and Benjamin White, 1769.

Martin, Charles Trice. *The Record Interpreter: A Collection of Abbreviations, Latin Words and Names Used in English Historical Manuscripts and Records* (2nd ed). London: Stevens and Sons, 1910.

Meekings, Cecil Anthony Francis. "The Pipe Roll Order of 12 February 1270." In *Studies Presented to Sir Hilary Jenkinson*, edited by James Conway Davies, 222–53. London: Oxford University Press, 1957.
Mills, Mabel H. "Correspondence: The Pipe Rolls After Henry III's Accession." *History NS* 11, 42 (1926): 141.
———. "Exchequer Agenda and Estimate of Revenue, Easter Term 1284." *EHR* 40, 158 (1925): 229–34.
———. "Experiments in Exchequer Procedure (1200–1232)." *TRHS* 8 (Fourth Series) (1925): 151–70.
———. "Review of James H. Ramsay, A History of the Revenues of the Kings of England, 1066–1399." *EHR* 41, 163 (1926): 429–31.
———. "The Reforms at the Exchequer (1232–1242)." *TRHS* 10 (Fourth Series) (1927): 111–33.
Mitchell, Sydney Knox. *Studies in Taxation Under John and Henry III*. New Haven: Yale University Press, 1914.
Morris, William Alfred. *The Early English County Court. An Historical Treatise With Illustrative Documents*. Berkeley: University of California Publications in History, 1926.
Ormrod, William Mark. "Royal Finance in Thirteenth-Century England." In *Thirteenth Century England V*, edited by Peter R. Coss and Simon D. Lloyd, 141–64. Woodbridge: Boydell Press, 1995.
Oschinsky, Dorothea. *Walter of Henley and Other Treatises on Estate Management and Accounting*. Oxford: Clarendon Press, 1971.
Page, Mark, and Matthew Bristow, eds. *A History of the County of Northampton. Volume VII, Corby and Great Oakley* (Victoria County History). London: Published for the Institute of Historical Research by Boydell & Brewer, 2013.
Pipe Roll Society. *Introduction to the Study of the Pipe Rolls*. Vol. 3 London: Pipe Roll Society, 1884.
Poole, Reginald L. *The Exchequer in the Twelfth Century*. Oxford: Clarendon Press, 1912.
Prestwich, Michael. *War, Politics and Finance Under Edward I*. London: Faber and Faber, 1972.
Public Record Office. *List of Foreign Accounts Enrolled on the Great Rolls of the Exchequer* (Lists and Indexes No. 11). London: HMSO, 1900.
———. *Prospectus for the Publication of a Calendar of Pipe Rolls, Henry III*. London: HMSO, 1949.
Röhrkasten, Jens. "The General Eyre and Royal Finance." In *Law and Society in Later Medieval England and Ireland*, edited by Travis R. Baker. London: Routledge, 2018.
Sabapathy, John. *Officers and Accountability in Medieval England, 1170–1300*. Oxford: Oxford University Press, 2014.
Sanders, Ivor John. *English Baronies: A Study of Their Origin and Descent 1086–1327*. Oxford: Clarendon Press, 1960.
Stacey, Robert C. "Agricultural Investment and the Management of the Royal Demesne Manors, 1236–1240." *Journal of Economic History* 46, 4 (1986): 919–34.
———. *Politics, Policy, and Finance Under Henry III, 1216–1245*. Oxford: Clarendon Press, 1987.
Stenton, Doris Mary. "The Pipe Rolls and the Historians, 1600–1883." *Cambridge Historical Journal* 10, 3 (1952): 271–92.

Vincent, Nicholas. *Peter Des Roches: An Alien in English Politics, 1205–1238*. Cambridge Studies in Medieval Life and thought. Cambridge: Cambridge University Press, 1996.

Watts, Victor E. *The Cambridge Dictionary of English Place-Names: Based on the Collections of the English Place-Name Society*. Cambridge: Cambridge University Press, 2004.

Waugh, Scott L. "The Origins of the Office of Escheator." In *The Growth of Royal Government under Henry III*, edited by David Crook and Louise J. Wilkinson, 227–65. Woodbridge: Boydell Press, 2015.

Wilkinson, Louise J. "Women as Sheriffs in Early Thirteenth Century England." In *English Government in the Thirteenth Century*, edited by Adrian Jobson, 111–24. Woodbridge: Boydell Press, The National Archives, 2004.

Online sources

"An Introduction to Pipe Rolls." *Pipe Roll Society*. https://piperollsociety.co.uk/contents-and-use.

"Anglo-American Legal Tradition [AALT]." http://aalt.law.uh.edu/index.htm.

"Calendar of the Fine Rolls of the Reign of Henry III [CFR]." https://finerollshenry3.org.uk/content/calendar/calendar.html.

"Discovery." *The National Archives*. https://discovery.nationalarchives.gov.uk.

"Henry III Fine Rolls Project." https://finerollshenry3.org.uk/home.html.

"Medieval Financial Records: Pipe Rolls 1130-c. 1300." *The National Archives*. www.nationalarchives.gov.uk/help-with-your-research/research-guides/medieval-financial-records-pipe-rolls-1130-1300/.

"Oxford Dictionary of National Biography." www.oxforddnb.com.

"Some Notes on Medieval English Genealogy." www.medievalgenealogy.org.uk/index.html.

"Survey of English Place-Names." https://epns.nottingham.ac.uk.

Index

abbreviations in pipe rolls 7, 19
accountability of officials 4–5, 39–40, 42–3, 64–5
adventus 16–17, 56, 58–9; definition 82
aids 38; definition 82
amercements 17, 34–5, 52–5, 67–8; definition 82
Anglo-American Legal Tradition (AALT) 20–1, 46, 55
attermination 30, 50, 54; definition 82
audit 3, 59–60; timetable 56–7

Barratt, Nick 23
beaupleder fines 34; definition 82
blanching of payments 11, 30–1, 49; definition 82
boroughs: farm of 32–4, 50, 56
building works 64

calendar of pipe rolls 20
carucage 37; definition 82
chancellor's rolls 17, 19; definition 82; difference from pipe rolls 18
Chancery 17, 53, 56; definition 82
communia *see* memoranda rolls
compendium rolls 74; definition 82
corpus comitatus 31, 47, 71–3; calculation of 52; definition 82
county courts 32–3, 35, 52–3
county farm 30–2, 47, 52, 72–3; definition 82
Crook, David 23
custodian sheriffs 24, 32–3, 47, 50; definition 82
customs 42–3

dates in pipe rolls 11; saints' days 11–12; *see also* regnal years
debts: and payments 29; removed from pipe rolls 70–1; *see also* desperate debts
debts and liberties 54, 68
De oblatis 8, 49, 59; definition 84
desperate debts 70, 73; definition 83
Dialogue of the Exchequer 21; unreliability for 13th century 22
dies dati 16–17, 56–7; definition 83
distraint 59; definition 83
dividend payments 56, 58
dividend tally 24, 68; definition 83

Edward I (lord Edward) 34, 36, 38
Edward II 69, 74–5
escheators 42, 63; definition 83
estreats 17, 24, 54–5, 69, 73–4; definition 83
exannual rolls 72; definition 83
exchanges 41; definition 83
Exchequer 33; definition 83; limitations of accounts 42–3; marshal of 60; role 3–4; terms 13; year 12
Exchequer of Pleas 74
Exchequer records *see* issue rolls; liberate rolls; memoranda rolls; particulars of account; pipe rolls; receipt rolls
expenditure 31, 48, 61, 64
eyres 8, 34, 54–5, 67–9; definition 83

family history 62–5
famine 60

Index

farmer sheriffs 31–3, 50; definition 83
fine rolls 17, 35, 53–4, 62
fines 35, 53–4; definition 83
fixed alms 30, 48; definition 83
foreign accounts 15, 75; contents 39–42; definition 83; growth of 39; introduction of 38–9
fractional taxes 36

gold 10, 62–3
great rolls *see* pipe rolls

headings 8
Henry III 10, 24, 34, 36, 38, 40–1, 61–4
hundred courts 32–3, 35, 52–3; definition 83
Hunter, Joseph 19

increment 32; definition 83
instalments *see* attermination
Ireland 40, 43
issue rolls 16; definition 83

Jewish community 36, 43
John, king 12, 35, 37
justice: profits of 32–4, 52–5; *see also* amercements; county courts; eyres; hundred courts

knights' fees 37

Latin in pipe rolls 6
liberate rolls 16–17, 64; definition 84
local history 62–5
lump sum payments 24, 36, 54–5, 57–8, 67–8, 70, 73

Madox, Thomas 22–3
Magna Carta 24, 36–7, 63
manors: accounts for 42; farm of 25, 32–4, 39, 51
marginal notes 49–50, 54–5, 68–9
marks 10
marriage 62–3
Meekings, C.A.F. 25
memoranda rolls 16, 55–7, 73; communia 16; county accounts in 16, 59–60; definition 84
Mills, Mabel 22, 24, 42
money 9–10, 41; units 10

Norman pipe rolls 43
Northamptonshire county account 47–50
Northumberland pipe rolls 20
Nova oblata 8, 35, 49, 53, 62–3, 69; definition 84
numerals 8–9

originalia rolls 17, 24, 35, 53–4, 56, 69, 73; definition 84
Oxfordshire account examples 77–81

particulars of account 17, 24, 33, 52; definition 84
Pipe Roll Order 1270 71–2
pipe rolls: background 15; description 3–5; in English 20; example of 1259 46–65; online 20–1; reading 5, 18; reference to 73–5; size of rolls 16, 18; timetable for production 55–7; years 12–13; *see also* debts
Pipe Roll Society 19–20, 23, 25, 46, 77
place-names 47
Poole, R.L. 23
profit 32, 48, 52, 56, 58, 64; definition 84

queen's wardrobe 41

receipt rolls 16; chronological 57–8; definition 84; three-column 57–8
Record Commission 19
record type 19; definition 84
reform of government 32–3, 55, 60–1
regnal years 11–12, 46; definition 84
relief 63–4; definition 84
rotulets: definition 4, 84; order of 57
rotuli compotorum see foreign accounts
rotulus de corporibus 72–4; definition 84
rotulus pullorum 70–1; definition 85
royal demesne 15, 25, 32, 34; definition 83; farming of 33; *see also terre date*
royal household 40–1; *see also* Wardrobe

scutage 8, 36–7; definition 85
sheriff's account 30–1; *see also corpus comitatus*

sheriffs: appointment 55–6; oath 56; women sheriffs 33; *see also* county farm; custodian sheriffs; sheriff's account
Stacey, Robert 23, 25
Stapeldon, Walter 75
statute of Rhuddlan 72
sum 60
summons 16, 56, 69, 71; definition 85
Surrey pipe roll 24

tallage 36, 74; definition 85
tally sticks 17, 67–8; definition 85; *see also* dividend tally
taxes 35–8, 43

tenants-in-chief 37, 42, 63–4; definition 85
terre date 30, 32–3, 47–8, 52, 62, 72–3; definition 85
transcription conventions 77

vacancies 41, 56, 58, 61, 75; definition 85
view of account 56

Wardrobe 10, 12, 39, 51, 62; definition 85; failure to account 40–1, 43
Watford, Eustace of 47–8, 50, 58–9
Winchester castle 64

For Product Safety Concerns and Information please contact our EU representative GPSR@taylorandfrancis.com
Taylor & Francis Verlag GmbH, Kaufingerstraße 24, 80331 München, Germany

www.ingramcontent.com/pod-product-compliance
Lightning Source LLC
Chambersburg PA
CBHW051758230426
43670CB00012B/2345